Pioneers in Gardening

Pioneers in Gardening

MILES HADFIELD

BLOOMSBURY

BLOOMSBURY GARDENING CLASSICS

Editorial Advisory Board

Montagu Don
Peter King

This edition first published in Great Britain 1996
Bloomsbury Publishing Plc, 2 Soho Square, London W1V 6HB

Copyright © 1995 The Estate of Miles Hadfield

The moral right of the author has been asserted

First published 1955

A CIP catalogue record for this book is available
from the British Library

ISBN 0 7475 2956 6

10 9 8 7 6 5 4 3 2 1

Typeset by Hewer Text Composition Services, Edinburgh
Printed by Clays Limited, St Ives plc

CONTENTS

ILLUSTRATIONS

INTRODUCTION

Before beginning the story of pioneers we should settle one or two special problems which the subject sets.

First, what is a pioneer? It is not difficult to define this when we are talking about the history of a science. If we discuss the pioneers of electricity, for instance, and follow the history of this subject we find that it develops gradually from the simplest experiments, becoming more and more complicated as the years pass until it is now that vast body of science and engineering which provides much of the world with heat, light and power. Progress has gone forward step by step, and each of the important steps has been the result of the activities of one man. Thus, at the end of the eighteenth century an Italian, Alessandro Volta, pioneered with a simple, primitive electric battery. Then, in 1831, an Englishman, Michael Faraday, made another pioneering discovery. "Think I have got hold of a good thing," he wrote; it was the principle from which the dynamo soon developed. And in our own century, another Italian, Marconi, this time working in England, making the experiments that pioneered radio, with all its complexity, far removed from Volta's little battery. We have no difficulty in naming the pioneers.

We could do the same in writing about botany, the study of plants, or perhaps even horticulture, which is the practical science of making plants grow. But gardening, in addition to consisting of a little botany and more horticulture, includes also the design and making of gardens, a matter which is nearer to art than science and about which there is no finality. Gardening is not one thing but many: most of the greatest gardens that the world has ever known are things of the past, yet in many ways we now know more about horticulture, and certainly much more of botany, than at any time since man became interested in them.

Geography gives another instance of how different gardening is from science. Science is international: a botanist in tropical Africa can study and follow exactly the same subject (by means of the international botanical language of Latin) as one in London or New York. But gardens and gardening are so dependent on geography—climate in particular—that in the tropics they are absolutely different from in Europe. This works in another way too. The climates of some parts of the world, though remote from each other, are not very dissimilar. For example, parts of China have weather not much unlike that on the western side of the British Isles. The trees, shrubs and plants growing wild in those parts of China (its native flora) are infinitely more numerous and colourful than our own modest wild flowers. In the last century intrepid and skilful plant collectors have visited these remote places and brought many of the plants back with them. The gardens of the British Isles and other parts of the world with similar climates have consequently been enriched beyond belief by these foreign (or exotic) plants, which are quite hardy here; indeed, some grow better than they do at home.

Yet all these wonders have come to us in an age when the greatest gardens man has known belong to history and exist no more!

There is one more point that shows the difficulty: the everlasting battle between the formal and informal (or natural) design of gardens. The one, all rulers and, compasses, avenues, straight canals, terraces and steps; the other, irregular curves, gentle banks and purling streams. Neither is "better" than the other; at one point in the story one style is triumphant, at another period the other.

In fact, what we call gardening is a mixture consisting of a small part science, a part art (or perhaps more accurately a sort of architecture) and a large part of growing plants. It makes no steady sort of progress through history to any fixed goal of perfection, but wanders happily about, pursuing different ends in different ages. In one century the great formal garden has its triumph, so we must take as one pioneer the famed designer Le Nôtre. Another has as its feature the first realisation by gardeners that many kinds of foreign plants are desirable and will flourish; so that we shall discuss the adventurous pioneers of plant collection in the wild parts of the world, men such as Robert Fortune and David Douglas. We shall follow a zigzag course in choosing heroes, some more or less architects, some scientists, others founders of great botanic gardens—and some merely great gardeners.

One point about the manner in which we shall display and discuss them. "Personalities" are all the fashion these days: what great people wear, what they eat and how they behave are "all the news". Many of those who write about the great people of the past have patiently and cleverly routed out the most minute details of what their heroes and heroines did in their daily life, how they looked and behaved. The result is quite often rather flattering to you and me: the great ones turn out to be no better as persons than we are. But this method of turning heroes into ordinary people has one big fault: it tends to make us overlook the real difference between them and us—that is, the significant buildings they designed, the pictures they painted, the music they composed or the gardens they made. All these are quite beyond our capacity. Therefore, I shall try and lay emphasis on the *achievements* of pioneers rather than on their private lives, for it is these alone that make them worth while studying.

And I shall try to give just a hint of the background against which they worked. As history is not just a list of kings, queens, battles and treaties with dates attached, but the every-day things that happened between whiles, so gardening is always closely connected with the arts and sciences, and particularly the fashions, of the day.

ACKNOWLEDGEMENTS

I am grateful to the Editor of *Gardening Illustrated* (a paper founded by one of our pioneers, William Robinson) for allowing me to use my drawing of *Primula sieboldii* which he published.

CHAPTER 1

The Very Beginning

It is not surprising that the legends in which the great religious faiths of man are cradled nearly always tell us of gardens—paradises that existed towards the beginning of time. None is more significant than the story with which the Christian faith begins. This tells how, immediately after the creation of the world, "God planted a garden eastward in Eden; and there he put the man whom he had formed." So it was Adam, the first man of all, who was for Christians the first gardener, working in Eden "to dress it and to keep it". We remember, too, that his first-born child was Cain, a "tiller of the ground", and not Abel, the "keeper of sheep". These two men might stand as symbols of the first pioneers, whose names are unknown, but who have tackled the trees and herbs in the wilderness, bringing them into order and from them enticing food for our nourishment and beauty for our delight.

Greek mythology tells of gardens nearer home. There was, for instance, that lying around the home of the three Hesperides—those nymphs, daughters of Hesperus, the evening star. Here grew fruits of the most delicious kinds, none more so than the golden apples for which Hercules sought. Who was the gardener there we are not told; may it have been the dragon Ladon, who never slept, so great was his vigilance to prevent strangers entering and taking the fruit? He was certainly like some gardeners we can remember.

The Eastern religions also have their fabulous gardens. They play a singular part in the Buddhist religion. Both the Chinese and Japanese have been skilled gardeners from early times. Their temple grounds are sanctuaries for trees—notably the ancient maidenhair tree or ginkgo, which the priestly gardeners have saved from extinction (for it is nowhere found growing wild). It is recorded that some years ago a party of Buddhist priests from Japan were visiting England. One late afternoon they were taken up the Malvern Hills. In the evening, descending towards the setting sun, they paused spellbound: the scene was, they said, so like the ancient garden described in their religious books.

Unhappily for our stories, all the evidence collected by archaeologists goes to show that gardening did not come into being until long after man appeared on the world's scene. In the days of primitive humans, the hunter seems to have come before the farmer—and, of course, the farmer precedes the gardener. We look in vain, for instance, at the Abbé Breuil's many copies of the strange and often beautiful wall paintings done by prehistoric man on the cave walls of France and Spain for representations of plants; we see nothing but beasts and men. Examinations of the remains of ancient camps in northern Europe show that their inmates fed on meat—deer and aurochs—living wild in the forests. Not until later, when the Neolithic Revolution took place, did the farmer come along—the man who cleared patches of forest by burning and then fed meagrely on the fruits and seeds of the wild plants that sprang up. Perhaps, therefore, one should choose some unknown man of that period as the first real pioneer.

Or one might choose Alcinous, King of the Phaecians. Homer tells us how Ulysses visited his garden, planted on what is now the island of Corfu.

> Four acres was th' allotted space of ground,
> Fenc'd with a green enclosure all around.
> Tall thriving trees confess'd the fruitful mould;
> The red'ning apple ripens here to gold,
> Here the blue fig with luscious juice o'erflows,
> With deeper red the full pomegranate glows,
> The branch here bends beneath the weighty pear,
> And verdant olives flourish round the year.

A garden to make your mouth water! Unfortunately we don't really know very much about it, nor of the gardeners who kept it. But we can go back a long way in the history of European gardens. There is plenty of evidence that gardening in the sense that we know it today—something connected with recreation and pleasure, in addition to the utilitarian cultivation of food—existed sixteen hundred years before the birth of Christ. Discoveries on the island of Crete (not so very far from Corfu) give us a good idea of gardens at that period. Wall paintings have there been found showing gardens and parks. Avenues are to be seen too. Yet perhaps most interesting are the Cretan paintings of individual flowers. The iris can be identified, as also the crocus and Madonna lily. Possibly the rose is also shown, though some experts say that this is the rock-rose.

But we must turn from these hazy scenes of antiquity with their mythical figures, and find more solid beings.

Three or four centuries before the birth of Christ, Athens was the centre which held Plato and Aristotle while Alexander the Great with his army was striding into Asia and bringing back a wealth of new knowledge. That was the world into which Theophrastus was born at Eresos in the island of Lesbos, about 373 BC. His father was a fuller—a worker in the making of cloth. The son, therefore, had behind him a background of practical work; this helped to give the practical bent to his future labour, great thinker though he was. Going to Athens as a young man, he studied under Plato at the Academy. Working at the Academy with Theophrastus was Aristotle, one of the first great thinkers to approach the problems of the world in a scientific manner—perhaps because he was the son of a doctor and knew something at first hand of the processes of nature. Eventually Aristotle broke away from the Academy to found a new place of study, his Lyceum. Here Theophrastus joined him and, on his death, became its head. The years during which these two men ruled over the Lyceum were immensely important. They saw the publication of philosophical and scientific works upon which little advance was made for centuries.

Theophrastus is generally called the Father of Botany, since, in addition to much else, he wrote a remarkable work called *An Enquiry Into Plants*. He was also a practical gardener, and wrote frequently on garden plants; he is, therefore, certainly entitled to one of the early places in this book.

The *Enquiry* gives a picture of the knowledge of plant life in the Greek world of those days. Further, Theophrastus used the reports made by the learned men taken by Alexander, to observe the life of the Asian countries into which his expeditions penetrated. And finally, Theophrastus learned from his master Plato that to study things it was necessary to classify them. The *Enquiry* is, therefore, the first known attempt at the classification of plants.

From his will we learn that he kept his own garden. There he studied the plants about which he wrote. No doubt, too, he grew some of those plants that came back with Alexander; we can imagine him patiently waiting for the moment when they would first flower. Most interesting is his will. This makes arrangements for the maintenance of this garden after his death. It was left to certain of his friends so that they and others might use it as they had during his lifetime for the pursuit of learning and philosophy. In it his mortal remains were to be buried with a ceremony that was to be simple and without extravagance. He also instructed that a custodian be appointed to maintain the garden. Finally, provision was made for freeing the labouring slave gardeners when they had given good and long service. He was clearly a devoted gardener.

Few books have been more fortunate in their English translator than the *Enquiry Into Plants*. He was Sir Arthur Hort, not only a distinguished Greek scholar but an enthusiastic, skilful and learned amateur gardener.

Theophrastus wrote first of the roses known to the Greeks. He tells us that there are several kinds, differing in the number of their petals. Some have five, others twelve or twenty, some even a hundred. They differ, too, in their colour and sweetness of scent—not all, indeed, are fragrant. Some are "rough" (thorny) while others are smooth-stemmed. We learn that the sweetest came from Cyrene (in North Africa), and that roses flower after the polyanthus, narcissus, anemone and corn flag (a kind of gladiolus). One other interesting fact has been remarked upon by those who have studied the book closely: red roses were unknown to Theophrastus; only white and pink kinds were grown in Greece.

Turning to another page, we see him writing as a practical gardener.

The gilliflower, he tells us, lives at the most for three years; even so, with age it degenerates and the flowers become paler. A rose-bush, however, will live for five years, after which its prime is past, unless it be pruned.

Elsewhere he relates that position and the right climate most affect the fragrance of gilliflowers and other plants; in Egypt (so he has been assured), while all other flowers are without smell, the myrtles are marvellously fragrant. In that country, too, gilliflowers and other kinds bloom as much as two months earlier than they do in Greece, and they last longer, or certainly as long, in flower.

We can see from this that the talk of gardeners has changed but little in its kind over the centuries!

From Greece we must go forward to Rome of the first century after the birth of Christ—the period of the notorious Nero and the more respected Vespasian. There lived Caius Plinius Secundus, commonly called Pliny the naturalist. Whether or not he was a gardener I do not know, but he must be mentioned as the author of *The Natural History*—a book which today would probably be called an encyclopaedia, so wide is its range. It does, however, give us a great deal of information about the plants of the Romans and the gardens in which they were grown.

Of Pliny himself not very much is known. An inquiring naturalist to the last, he lost his life when studying the eruption of Vesuvius in A.D. 79; it seems that he had become asthmatic in old age and that the fumes given off by the volcano overcame him.

Pliny's work had the fortune to be translated into English during the reign of Queen Elizabeth I by Philemon Holland, "Doctor in Physicke". *The Historie of the World, Commonly called The Naturall Historie of C. Plinius Secundus,* as he called his translation, is a lively and entertaining book.

Pliny tells us much more about the rose than Theophrastus; he describes twelve kinds—a bright red rose among them.

From him we also gather that the Romans, as with so much else, took over the arts of gardening as known to others and developed them enormously. Flowers were grown to be woven into garlands appropriate to every sort of occasion. As Pliny says (in the words of Philemon Holland), it is ordained as a necessary point of gardens

> "that they should be planted and enriched with such hearbes as might bring forth flowers for coronets and guirlands . . . Whereas Dame Nature hath unto those fruits of the earth which serve for necessities and the sustentation of man long life, even to last yeares, and hundreds of yeares; these flowers of pleasure and delight, good only to content the eye or please the sence of smelling, she would have to live and die in one day. A great document and lesson for us men in generall to learn."

To give an idea of the manner in which the Roman gardener thought about his plants, here is another quotation, this time about the lily:

> "Next to the Rose, there is not a fairer flower than the Lillie, nor of greater estimation. The oiles also and ointments made of them both, have a resemblance and an affinitie one to the other. As touching the oile of Lillies, the Physicians call it Lirinon. And if a man should speak truly, a Lillie growing among Roses, becommeth and beautifieth the place very well; for it beggineth then to flower when the Roses have halfe done. There is not a flower in the garden again that groweth taller than the Lillie, reaching otherwhile to the height of three cubits from the ground: but a weak and slender necke it hath, and carrieth it not streight and upright, but it bendeth and noddeth downeward, as being not of strength sufficient to beare the weight of the head standing upon it. The flower is of incomparable whitenes, devided into leaves, which without-forth are chamfered, narrowed at the bottome, and by little and little spreading broader toward the top: fashioned all together in manner of a broad mouthed cup or beaker, the brims and lips whereof turne up somewhat backward round about and lie very open. Within these leaves there appeare certaine fine threads in manner of seeds: and just in the middest stand yellow chives, like as in Saffron.

"Now Lillies be set and sowed after the same manner in all respects as the roses, and grow as many waies. This vantage moreover they have of the roses, that they will come up of the very liquor that distilleth and droppeth from them, like as the hearb Alisanders: neither is there in the world an hearb more fruitfull, insomuch as you shall have one head of a root put forth oftentimes five hundred bulbs or cloves".

What a delightful piece of careful observation—ending in that flight of pure fancy when we are solemnly assured that young plants will spring up from the nectar that drips from the flowers!

In Europe the interest in gardens and gardeners (apart from the cultivation of fruit and vegetables) was at first and for a long time of rather a different kind from our own. Apart from the flowers grown for garlands, gardeners (and writers about gardens and plants) were more concerned with the healing qualities of the flowers that they grew than with their beauty. The "virtues" of plants were of great importance. Usually these were medicinal qualities, and we should not forget that in the times before proper drainage and baths a strong-smelling plant might have its uses.

Thus it is that much that we know of gardens and plants from early days until Elizabethan times is found in books called "herbals". These were written primarily to enlighten men about the medicinal uses and virtues of plants, how to cultivate them and, of course, how to identify them—for mistakes might have disastrous results.

The greatest herbal of all was one compiled during the same century that Pliny lived. The author was Pedanios Dioscorides. Not much is known about him. He lived at Anazarba, a town in Cilicia, which on a modern map lies on the mainland to the north of Cyprus and south of the Taurus Mountains. It seems that he was at one time a soldier, probably serving as a physician with the Roman army. Later he settled down as a writer. His book, usually called *The Greek Herbal*, was a standard work for fifteen hundred years. During the present century monks of the ancient community of Mount Athos in Greece still made use of it to identify medicinal herbs and their uses.

Although most old English authors quoted or adapted Dioscorides time and time again, no complete English translation of his *Herbal*

was published until the twentieth century. The version then issued
had been made three hundred years before by John Goodyer for his
own use. (Goodyer himself will concern us later, at the time of the
Civil War, as one of the pioneers who by the introduction of scientific
methods ousted Dioscorides and his *Herbal* from the scene.)

The *Herbal*, however, long reigned supreme. It covered a vast range:
aromatics, ointments, trees, fruit trees, milk and dairy produce, cereals,
metallic ores, wines and vines all come into it. And living creatures: here
is what he wrote about the lark: "The Larck is but a little bird, having
upon ye top of his head a tuff standing up, like to that of a peacock.
This bird being eaten roasted is good for such as are troubled with ye
colick." Delightful though the description is, we must never forget that
Dioscorides is thinking first and foremost about those "troubled with
ye colick". Even when he comes to describe the rose, he tells us that
"the flower found in the middest of the roses (the bundle of stamens)
being dry'd and sprinkled on, is good for the fluxes of the gummes."

To give us an idea of the attitude of an intelligent man of two
thousand years ago towards garden plants it may be well to quote *The
Greek Herbal* rather more fully, this time modernising the language.
We will take for example a well-known flower, the bearded iris:

> "This plant is called by some *Iris illyrica*, some *Thelpida*,
> while other names used are *Urania, Catharon, Gladiolus,
> Opertitis* and *Consecratix*; the Romans call it *Radix Marica*
> and the Egyptians *Nar*. It is named Iris from the resemblance
> to the rainbow in heaven. The leaves are like a little sword,
> but broader and thicker. The flowers are bended in, one
> over against another, and are of diverse colours, white or
> pale-coloured, black, purple or azure; from this variety of
> colours it is likened to the rainbow. The roots are knotty,
> stout and sweetly scented. After cutting, they ought to be
> dried in the shade, bound round with linen thread, and stored.
> The best roots are those coming from Macedonia and Illyria.
> These have a thick, stumpy root, which is tough to break, pale
> yellow in colour, sweetly scented but very bitter to the taste;
> when grinding them up they will make you sneeze.
>
> "Second best are those that come from Libya, which are

white and bitter. They become worm-eaten with age, but in this state they are more sweetly scented.

"All iris roots have a warm, soothing faculty, excellent to use for coughs. They purge thick humors and choler. If drunk in seven drams of hydromel they cause sleep, provoke tears, and heal torments of the belly. Drunk with vinegar they help such as are bitten by venomous beasts, those suffering from the spleen, those troubled with convulsions, such as are chilled and stiff with cold, and such as let fall their food."

One should add that Illyria and Macedonia are now the western coastal lands and the eastern part of Jugoslavia; that Libya is on the coast of northern Africa; that "humors and choler" and "the spleen" are phrases for the condition we call liverish; and that hydromel is a mixture of honey and water.

What a curious mixture of accurate observation, fact and nonsense! Yet it is typical of most that was written about plants until the sixteenth century, and shows how their healing properties were uppermost in the minds of all gardeners.

I doubt whether from the time of Dioscorides to the end of the fifteenth century we can find any real pioneers in gardening; the great names belong rather to the slow development of medicine and first attempts at botany. Nor can I find much about the individual pioneers in China and Japan, countries where gardening is of great antiquity: Marco Polo, the Venetian who in the thirteenth century made a long stay in China at the court of Kubla Khan and visited Japan, tells us nothing about the gardens.

But some space should be given to Mexico. When Cortes invaded the land in the sixteenth century, his reports were full of admiration; he wrote about "many trees and sweet scented flowers", orchards and terraces, roses and flowering shrubs. The Emperor Montezuma himself had laid out some of these gardens; he and his predecessors were certainly pioneers. Their gardens had many resemblances to those of our own day and had features quite unusual in sixteenth-century Europe. For instance, he laid out pleasure gardens in high places so that he might admire the sweeping distant views—whereas the European garden of the time kept itself privately between walls. The gardens that

Montezuma liked best, however, were smaller, and contained nothing but aromatic and medicinal herbs, flowers, native roses and trees with fragrant blossoms.

One remarkable garden was that built on the hill of Chapultepec. At its base were planted groves of the water cypress—or *Taxodium* (a tree which can often be seen in Britain, notably by the lake in Kew Gardens). The top of the hill was again wooded, but with other trees. In between these bands of woodland were terraces. These were something like our modern rock-gardens, the artful Mexican gardeners having apparently learned that many plants thrive when their roots run under stones.

The flowers that grew in these Mexican gardens must have made a dazzling display. Many were brought to Europe years afterwards, and provide us with some of our gayest half-hardy bedding-out plants—such as zinnias and dahlias. Orchids and those brilliant bulbs tigridias were also common—along with many native trees and shrubs that are highly ornamental.

Remains of these old gardens, including some of the trees planted in the fifteenth century, survived until recent times; perhaps here and there some traces may still be found.

In Europe during the Middle Ages the art of gardening spread northwards from the Mediterranean countries; even so, in Britain it must have been largely restricted to the palaces and castles of the great and to the monasteries. With the coming of the Tudors, and particularly during and after the reign of Henry VIII, it progressed faster, and a few names of individuals begin to appear. There was William Turner, for example—generally called the "father of English botany". He was a clergyman, generally in trouble with the authorities on account of his obstreperous nature. In 1548 he published *Names of Herbes*, the first reasonably accurate list of trees, shrubs and plants growing in this country. He lived for a time at Kew, when he was in the service of the Lord Protector Somerset at neighbouring Syon; it is generally believed that he was responsible for the planting of some of the trees there.

We should say a word, too, about Thomas Hill, though we only know one fact about him—that he wrote the first gardening book to be published in England. Just about the year in which Queen Elizabeth I came to the throne appeared *A most briefe and pleasaunte treatise*

teachyng how to dresse, sowe and set a garden; and what remedies
also may be had and used agaynst suche beastes, wormes, flies; and
such like that noye gardens . . . This book, now extremely rare, was
like many others of that period, nothing very original, but taken from
authors writing in those European countries whose culture was more
advanced than our own.

The first truly English pioneer is John Gerard. His *Herball*, first
issued in 1597, is still a well-known and often-quoted book, but as
we shall see, it is both unreliable and something of a fraud.

Gerard was born at Nantwich in Cheshire in 1545. He came
to London, and was a barber-surgeon, a curious combination of
professions usual at that time. His right to be called a pioneer rests
neither on his profession nor his *Herball*, but because he was obviously
a clever gardener, and the first to make any adequate record of the plants
that he grew. He was in charge of the gardens of Elizabeth's treasurer,
Lord Burleigh, both in the Strand and at Theobalds in Hertfordshire.
He had also his own gardens at Holborn. There he brought together a
remarkable collection of plants, some of them quite unusual. In 1596 he
issued a catalogue of these plants. This is most important for historians,
as it includes the first mention that we have of many of the foreign
plants now growing in our gardens. Some no doubt had been here
for a number of years, while others he remarks upon as being recent
introductions.

It is worth mentioning that several gardening dictionaries give the
date at which foreign plants that we cultivate were introduced; a lot
were apparently brought over in the one year 1596—a rather odd
coincidence. The fact is, of course, that the dictionaries should say
"*before 1596*", since they make use of the earliest reference to the
plant, which happens to be in Gerard's catalogue of his Holborn
garden.

It is interesting to note some of Gerard's "new" plants and whence
they came. From furthest afield were the wrongly called African
marigold, native of Mexico, and the "love apple", or tomato, then
grown as a decorative plant and not for eating, which also came from
South America. From the Orient came the crown imperial, the first
hyacinths and the Judas tree. New plants from southern Europe were
the earliest florist's anemones, the first Michaelmas daisy, gladiolus,

lilac and philadelphus or mock orange. In Gerard, too, we find the first mention of dog's-tooth violets, winter aconites, grape hyacinths and the Madonna lily.

In the year following the issue of this interesting catalogue came his much more celebrated *Herball*. The story of this book is really a discredit both to Gerard and the printer and publisher, John Norton. It is as follows.

A famous Belgian botanist, Rembert Dodoens, had published in 1583 his collected works under the title of *Stirpium Historiae Pemptades Sex*. John Norton commissioned a certain Dr. Priest to translate this important work into English, but Priest died before he had finished the task. The whole business was then passed over to Gerard. He and Norton set about making it a "best-seller", which in those days meant that it was "principally intended for gentlewomen". To this end, Mrs. Gerard helped her barber-surgeon husband by advising him of the sort of things about which women liked to read. The worst feature of this publication, however, was that Gerard passed it off as his own work, whereas it is the *Pemptades* of Dodoens translated by Priest and Gerard—the contents, it is true, arranged in a different order, with some practical observations by Gerard the gardener added. To make matters worse, Norton bought what we should now call a job lot of wood engravings on the Continent to use for the illustrations. Gerard fitted these into his text, but knew so little about botany (as distinct from gardening) that he joined a number of the figures to the wrong text. Gerard was, alas, something of a liar too. We quite expect him to include the stories of legendary plants—for they crop up in all old books. But when he vouches for the truth of the barnacle goose plant from his own experience, we begin to wonder how far we can rely on anything he says:

> "But what our eies have seen, and hands have touched," he writes with seeming honesty, "we shall declare. There is a small island in Lancashire called the Pile of Foulders, wherein are found the broken pieces of old and brused ships, some whereof have beene cast thither by shipwrecke, and also the trunks or bodies with the branches of old and rotten trees, cast up there likewise: whereon is found a certain spume or froth,

that in time breedeth unto certaine shells, in shape like those
of the muskle, but sharper pointed, and of a whitish colour;
one ende whereof is fastned unto the inside of the shell, even
as the fish of oisters and muskles are; the other ende is made
fast unto the belly of a rude masse or lumpe, which in time
cometh to the shape and forme of a bird: when it is perfectly
formed, the shell gapeth open, and the first thing that apeereth
is the aforesaid lace or string; next come the legs of the bird
hanging out, and as it groweth greater, it openeth the shell by
degrees, till at length it is all come forth, and hangeth onely by
the bill; in short space after it commeth to full maturitie, and
falleth into the sea, where it gathereth feathers, and groweth
to a fowl, bigger than a mallard, and lesser than a goos."

Master Gerard! . . . what a story! Delightful, it is true, but throwing
a good deal of doubt upon other objects that he may claim to have
seen with his "eies" and touched with his hands.

However, when writing about garden plants nearer to hand than
on the "Pile of Foulders", we can assume that the *Herball* is reliable.
Gerard on roses, for example, is not only translating Dodoens but
adding something of his own knowledge; from him we gather the great
increase in the knowledge and cultivation of these shrubs since the days
of Rome. Let us quote some paragraphs by way of example:

"The rose doth deserve the chief and prime place among all
flowers whatsoever, being not onely esteemed for his beauty,
vertues, and his fragrant and odoriferous smell, but also
because it is the honour and ornament of our English Scepter,
as by the conjunction appeareth, in the uniting of those two
most Royall Houses of Lancaster and Yorke . .̖.

"If the curious could so be content, one generall description
might serve to distinguish the whole stock or kindred of the
roses being things so well known: notwithstanding I think
it not amiss to say something of them severally. The white
rose hath very long stalks of wooddy substance, set or armed
with divers sharpe prickles: the branches whereof are likewise
full of prickles, whereon grow leaves consisting of five leaves

for the most part, set upon a middle rib by couples, the odd leaf standing at the point of the same, and every one of those small leaves snipt about the edges, somewhat rough and of an overworne greene colour: from the bosome whereof shoot forth long foot-stalks, whereon grow very faire double flowers of a white colour, and a very sweet smell, having in the middle a few yellow threads or chives; which being past, there succeedeth a long fruit, greene at first, but red when it is ripe, and stuffed with a downy choking matter, wherein is contained seed as hard as stones. The root is long, tough, and of a wooddy substance.

"The red rose groweth very low in respect of the former: the stalks are shorter, smoother, and browner of colour: the leaves are like, yet of a worse dusty colour. The flowers grow on the tops of the branches, consisting of many leaves of a perfect red colour: the fruit is likewise red when it is ripe.

"The common damask rose in stature, prickely branches, and in other respects is like the white rose; the especiall difference consists in the colour and smell of the flowers: for these are of a pale red colour, of a more pleasant smell, and fitter for meat and medicine . . .

"The rose without prickles hath many young shoots comming from the root, dividing themselves into divers branches, tough, and of a wooddy substance as are all the rest of the roses, of the height of two or three cubits, smooth and plain without any roughnesse or prickles at all . . . The flowers grow at the tops of the branches, consisting of an infinite number of leaves, greater than those of the damask rose, more double, and of a colour between the red and the damask roses, of a most sweet smell . . .

"All these sorts of roses we have in our London gardens, except that rose without prickles, which as yet is a stranger in England. The double white rose groweth wilde in many hedges in Lancashire in great aboundance, even as briers do with us in these southerly parts."

Several other roses are similarly described. Of the yellow rose, for instance, Gerard tells us that people say the colour came from grafting a wild rose upon a yellow broom . . . "But for my part I having found the contrary by mine owne experience, cannot be induced to believe the report." He had, in fact, found by experiment that seeds and suckers from the root came true yellow.

Another interesting and no doubt quite authentic fact that he tells us is how the burnet rose "growes very plentifully in a field as you go from a village in Essex, called Graies (upon the brinke of the river Thames) unto Horndon . . . It groweth likewise in a pasture as you goe from a village hard by London, called Knightsbridge unto Fulham, a village thereby." From this we can see that it would not be so difficult in his time to grow choice plants in Holborn—then but a mile or two from the countryside.

So far as gardening is concerned, Gerard with all his failings is far in advance of any of his English predecessors. His book turned out to be the best-seller that its publisher had hoped, and there is no doubt that it advanced the popularity and study of gardening in England. He also made, but failed in, another attempt at pioneering. This was to establish the garden in which barber-surgeons might grow and become more thoroughly acquainted with their medicinal plants. Had his plan been put into practice, he would certainly have achieved great honour as the maker of the first botanic garden in Britain. But he died in 1607, and another fourteen years passed before England could vie with the Continent in this respect. The first botanic garden belongs to another chapter.

CHAPTER 2

John Goodyer and his Friends

We have seen that during the first Elizabethan age gardening became something much more than just growing fruit, herbs and vegetables, or plants from which medicines could be prepared. From the time of the death of Elizabeth to the start of the Civil War, there was great progress made, both in gardening and the study of plants. Charles I and his Queen, Henrietta Maria, were almost as much interested in gardening as in the other arts, and gave their support to several famous gardeners. Unhappily for the good both of gardening and botany, most of the pioneers were Royalists. Cromwell and his Puritans did not attract them, and during Cromwellian days gardening went into an eclipse, and the study of plants was carried on only quietly in places far from the tiresome Civil War.

Apart from the writings of some of these men, we do not know very much about their lives. But there is one exception. Until recent times among the shadowiest figures of them all was a certain John Goodyer. It was well enough known that he was an able botanist and gardener, but that was all. There had long been in the library of Magdalen College at Oxford a collection of his books and papers. I suppose they must have seemed an uninteresting lot—among them, for instance, were many business letters on the backs of which were written botanical notes. For this or some other reason, no one seems to have bothered to examine this mass of documents carefully until

R. T. Gunther, the librarian of the college, who was a keen student of the history of botany, decided to look more closely into it. The result was quite romantic. John Goodyer's habit of writing his botanical notes on the backs of letters enabled Mr. Gunther, when he had carefully transcribed both sides, to place them in their order of date. From the ordinary and business correspondence on one side, it was quite easy to build up the story of Goodyer's doings and business activities. The notes on the back recorded the progress of his studies and discoveries in botany and gardening. This habit of jotting down oddments on the backs of any letters that happened to be in his pocket at the time, together with many remarks and notes that he had added to the texts in his collection of books, enabled Mr. Gunther not only to bring Goodyer forward from the shadows and make him a very real and important person, but to give us many new sidelights on his friends and acquaintances.

He was born at Alton in Hampshire in 1592. His whole life was to be spent in the district—first as a young man at Droxford and then later at Petersfield. This is the same part of the world later to be described with such loving detail by the Rev. Gilbert White in *The Natural History of Selborne*, a parish which was but a few miles from all these homes of Goodyer. As White wrote, "the soils of this district are almost as various and diversified as the views and aspects"—quiet valleys of little rivers loved by fishermen, bare downs grazed by sheep, hills with hanging woods of beech and, not far away, the Wolmer Forest famous for its great oaks. Goodyer was therefore fortunate to be born where the variety of soils and situations makes for an equal richness of plant life.

He probably went to Alton Grammar School, and gained there a knowledge of Greek which was later put to good use as a translator.

The background of his youth must have been darkened by local events. Hampshire was then the home of many Roman Catholic families, some of fame and position, who were at that time subject to persecution. He would know, too, of the trial of Sir Walter Raleigh at Winchester near by—a trial of no credit to any but the remarkable spirit in whose execution, long years after the verdict was given, it resulted.

We next find him aged about twenty-four in the service of Sir

Thomas Bilson, a big landowner and man of affairs, of Mapledurham in Hampshire (not to be confused with the place having the same name in Berkshire). The young man seems to have been Bilson's agent, and frequently to have gone travelling about the countryside on his master's business. Possibly this was the cause of a long visit to London in 1616. While there, he bought some important books on botany, and made visits to distinguished botanists, gardeners and gardens.

We can realise how London has changed since those days if we name some of the gardens which Goodyer no doubt saw. At Westminster, Ralph Tuggy had "the best place for clove gilloflowers, pinks and the like"; in Long Acre, John Parkinson had already begun his garden which was soon to achieve lasting fame as "well stored with rarities" and from which Goodyer gathered seeds; there were Mr. Pemble's garden at "Marrybone" and Mr. Wilmot's at Bow, while John Millen of Old Street grew "the choicest fruits the Kingdom yields".

In addition to John Parkinson, Goodyer's particular gardening friend was William Coys.

Coys lived at Stubbers, in Essex, now on the fringe of London, a mile or two beyond Dagenham. The garden had been known to Gerard for its rare plants. Coys apparently had some connections with the New World, for he seems to have specialised in American plants. It was at Stubbers that the yucca, a native of eastern North America, first flowered in England in 1604. Goodyer made lists of his friend's plants which now provide historians with useful information about the early days of gardening. Mr. Gunther relates that some three hundred years later he was able to find William Coys' garden and see trees and plants that were no doubt descendants of those recorded by Goodyer.

In 1617 Goodyer was responsible for the distribution of the Jerusalem artichoke to our gardens. He tells us that "having received two small roots thereof from Master Franqueville of London no bigger than hen's eggs, the one I planted, the other I gave to a friend. Mine brought me a peck of roots, wherewith I stored Hampshire." Up to that time the only "Hartichoke", as it was called, known in England was the globe artichoke. Of this, the flower and not the root is eaten. Thus Droxford, where Goodyer then lived, has another claim to fame beyond its connections with Izaak Walton.

In the following years, during journeys in and around Hampshire, he tirelessly collected and described our native plants, recording the presence of many for the first time. He was, for instance, the original observer to note and describe the differences between our native elms. Although his library grew steadily, often he could not trace accounts of his finds, for the only reliable books that were published came from the Continent, and their authors had never seen a number of plants that grow only in England. As we have seen, Gerard's *Herball*, the only work in English, was little more than a translation from foreign authors, and the growing body of men interested in English plants came to realise that it was "imperfectly accommodated unto our English nation". So Goodyer worked away and made an invaluable collection of careful descriptions of the plants that he could nowhere find recorded. In the year 1621, for instance, he made records of at least ninety kinds—and was probably the first to recognise the fact that the yew normally carries the female flowers, which later turn into crimson berries, all on one tree, while the male flowers, which scatter their dusty pollen in February, are on separate trees. In 1625 we find him going further afield, to Northamptonshire, and making important discoveries there.

All this time he was in touch with many of the most eminent botanists and gardeners, and adding steadily to the collection of rare plants in his garden.

A most important event for Goodyer and his friends took place somewhere about 1628: "Tradescant's Ark" was opened.

THE TRADESCANTS

There were two Tradescants, both John—father and son (a grandson, also John, died as a young man). They were closely connected with Goodyer's friends, and few men played a more important part in the early history of gardening.

John Tradescant the elder came from East Anglia. We know little about him till we find that he married a Kentish girl at Meopham in 1607. He had met her while working at Shorne, an estate in that district owned by Robert Cecil, Earl of Salisbury and Lord Treasurer of England. Cecil was then building the great house at Hatfield which still stands. Among its archives are documents telling how Tradescant travelled on the Continent to buy all the best "routes, flowers, seedes, trees and plants" for the new garden. He visited Haarlem, Brussels and Leyden, bringing back new cherries, mulberries, "portingall" (Portugal) quince, "lion" quince, and that most exciting of all irises, *susiana*. In Paris he became friendly with Robin, the most eminent French gardener and herbalist after whom the false acacia or *Robinia* is named, and from there brought greenhouse fruits—pomegranates, grapes, peaches and figs.

On Cecil's death, he became gardener to Lord Wotton at St. Augustine's Palace, Canterbury. Soon he brought fame to the garden that he made there sheltering among the ruins of the old abbey, and where he got to know many famous men of the day who came to seek his advice. Probably through these connections, we find him investing his own money in an expedition to the developing new colony of Virginia, so that its members could bring him new plants that they found. One of them sent him what he believed to be "silk-grass" but which was that now popular spiderwort which bears his name.

Near to Canterbury lived Sir Dudley Digges. When he was sent by James I on a trade mission to the Emperor of Russia, Tradescant succeeded in joining the Party.

The mission was a costly failure for all concerned except its naturalist, who at Archangel mystified the Russians by his curiosity about plants that they considered weeds. He returned with a valuable load of plants and specimens of all kinds. Most important was a notebook full of descriptions that he had made, the first known list of Russian plants.

Tradescant next joined, as a "gentleman adventurer", an expedition against the Algerian corsairs. From it little harm came to the pirates, but at a good deal of risk to himself the "gentleman adventurer" made several trips ashore and so achieved his real ambition, which was, of course, to study plants and natural history. We can imagine the excitement of his friend Parkinson when he heard how Tradescant had seen in Barbary whole acres of the "corne flagge of Constantinople"—the gladiolus, rare at that time. He brought with him the once famous and luscious "Argiers apricocke"—an apricot which he propagated and which was soon in every nobleman's garden.

From Canterbury he entered the service of the Duke of Buckingham.

Letters still exist, written under Buckingham's name but clearly inspired by Tradescant, to the Secretary of the Admiralty, urging that expeditions to foreign parts should collect for him plants, birds, rare stones and objects of all sorts, ranging from a pair or two of young storks to an elephant's head with the teeth in it!

Tradescant later sailed with his master on the expedition to La Rochelle. In the disastrous campaign that followed, Tradescant at least earned credit for his services as an "engineer".

When Buckingham was murdered, Tradescant became royal gardener and settled at Lambeth, on the south side of the Thames. It was here that he opened his "Ark", which was in reality the first English museum. In it were displayed all the curios that he had collected. Outside was a garden full of rare trees and plants.

John the elder died in 1637 while John the younger was in Virginia collecting plants. The son came home and became successor to his father as gardener to Charles I. After the King's death, he devoted his life to the Ark and its garden. Here he worked unperturbed through the Civil Wars. He produced the great catalogue of his collections, with illustrations engraved beautifully by Wenceslaus Hollar.

In it are listed plants and trees, some noted as growing for the first time in Britain, from New England, Virginia, the Barbadoes, Constantinople, Spain, Persia, Africa and Tartary. The Ark itself included a dragon's egg, a dodo and "fleachains of three hundred links".

John the third died long before his father, who died in 1662 when the Ark passed to an antiquarian named Elias Ashmole. In turn, he left it to Oxford University, where today it has become the Ashmolean Museum. The garden was soon neglected and before long even the trees had disappeared.

The family is remembered in the name of a street, and in a lovely epitaph:

> Know, stranger, e'er thou pass, beneath this stone
> Lie John Tradescant, grandsire, father, son . . .
> These famous antiquarians that had been
> Both gardeners to the rose and lily Queen,
> Transplanted now themselves, sleep here; and when

Tradescantia, or spiderwort, introduced by and named after John
Tradescant the younger

Angels shall with their trumpets waken men,
And fire shall purge the world, these hence shall rise
And change their gardens for a Paradise.

JOHN PARKINSON

At about the same time as the opening of the Ark, another of
Goodyer's closest friends, John Parkinson, whom we have already
mentioned, stepped into fame. In 1629 was published his *Paradisi
in Sole Paradisus Terrestris, or a choice garden of all sorts of rarest
flowers, with their nature, place of birth, time of flowering, names, and
virtues of each plant, useful in physic, or admired for beauty.* The idea
that they should be "admired for beauty" introduced something quite
new in gardening. Holland's translation of Theophrastus on the rose,
quoted above, should be compared with Parkinson writing on what,
in his day, were considered lilies:

"Because the lilly is the more stately flower among many:
and amongst the wonderful variety of lillies, known to us in
these dayes, much more than in former times, whereof some
are white, others blush, some purple, others red or yellow,
some spotted, others without spots, some standing upright,
others hanging or turning downwards. The Crown Imperial
for his stately beautifulnesse, deserveth the first place in this
our garden of delight, to be here entreated of before all other
lillies."

The cultivation of plants for beauty and delight became important.
   We can also read a description of the way plants were used in
"knots", the fancy-shaped flower beds then popular:

"You may mingle roots in their planting, many of divers sorts
together, that they may give the more glorious show when they
are in flower. That you may do so, you may first observe the
several kinds of them that do flower at one and the same time,
and then place them in such order and so near one to another,
that their flowers appearing together of several colours, will

cause the more admiration in the beholders, Thus: the vernal crocus or saffron flowers of the spring, white, purple, yellow and striped, with some vernal colchicum or meadow saffron among them; some Dens Canis or dog's-teeth, and some of the small early leucojum or bulbous violet, all planted in some proportion as near one to another as is fit for them, will give such grace to the garden, that the place will seem like a piece of tapestry of many glorious colours, to increase every one's delight."

That is real gardening—the laying out of a small, fancily-designed bed, called a "knot", and filling it with spring flowers. It gives us an idea of what gardeners grew in the days of James I and Charles I.

Parkinson was still equally interested in the uses and histories of plants, as we shall see if we turn up his description of the leek.

"The old world", he writes, "as we find in Scripture, in the time of the children of Israel being in Egypt, and no doubt long before, fed much upon leeks, onions and garlic boiled with flesh; and the antiquity of the Gentiles relate the same manner of feeding on them, to be in all countries the like, which however our dainty age now refuseth wholly, in all sorts except the poorest; yet Muscovia and Russia use them, and the Turks to this day have them among their dishes at their tables, although they be Bashas, Cades, or Vainodas; that is to say, lords, Judges, or governor of countries and places. They are used with us also sometimes in Lent to make pottage, and as great and general feeding in Wales with the vulgar gentleman."

So this great book (*Paradisi in Sole* is a play on his name, "park-in-sun") describes plants (about a thousand of them) from a gardener's *and* a botanist's point of view, the first of many such in England. The author, who was probably born in Nottinghamshire in 1567, was appointed apothecary to James I, and on the publication of *Paradisi*, dedicated to Queen Henrietta Maria, was given by Charles I the title *Botanicus Regius Primarius*. He was friendly with all the many clever men of his day—but it is around the garden at Longacre, visited in its early days by Goodyer, that his life and work were centred.

THOMAS JOHNSON

Tradescant's ardent interest in Russian plants may well have stimulated Goodyer—there remain, for example, several letters from him to a man connected with the Muscovia Company which traded with Russia. That was in 1632—the year in which, on 15th November, he married Patience Crump, spinster, and shortly after moved to a house in the Spain at Petersfield—to which there is now fixed a plate in his commemoration.

From now on, Mr. Gunther tells us, Goodyer's botanical notes are mixed up with details of household errands and shopping lists.

In 1633 a corrected and enlarged version of Gerard's *Herball* was published. This was the work of his great friend Thomas Johnson. The new edition of the work altered it from a popular best-seller into something of importance. Two thousand eight hundred and fifty plants were described—more than in any previous herbal. Such faith had Goodyer in Johnson that he handed him his accumulation of notes and descriptions of newly discovered plants. It was not misplaced, for by all accounts this Yorkshireman would have been one of the great figures in the world of botany. He was a brave and fearless man and, like most of his circle, had no doubt that the King's cause was right. In his early forties, as Lt.-Col. Johnson, a Royalist soldier of exceptional bravery, he was killed in the defence of Basing Castle, in Hampshire—the very county that was Goodyer's home. So ended far too early the life of a man "no less eminent as a soldier than as herbarist or physician". In his early days, when he kept an apothecary's shop in London, he had exhibited the first bananas ever seen in this country. They came from Bermuda; this historic display was on 10th April, 1633.

The miseries and disturbances of the Civil War must have weighed heavily on Goodyer. As a Royalist, the defeat of his cause would sadden him. Difficult conditions in the countryside cut short his botanising. Probably he spent much time among the friendly surroundings of Oxford.

When peace came, Goodyer found himself the most prominent and reliable botanist and gardener in the country—a position he would not have grudged Johnson had he lived to succeed to the fame of Parkinson, who died in 1650. In those years, too, he saw a widely increased interest in gardening and botany which no doubt delighted him.

At this period (in fact, to be precise, a note in his hand says at 11 a.m. on 10th March, 1655) he undertook a stupendous task. He copied out the Greek text of the *Materia Medica* of Dioscorides and translated it into English. His manuscript fills six volumes and 4,540 pages; we have read something about it earlier as *The Greek Herbal*.

That was his last big undertaking. His final years seem to have been spent largely in giving the benefit of his now vast knowledge of plants and their uses to others—particularly of their medicinal value to his ailing neighbours. He died in 1664.

CHAPTER 3

The Formal Garden

To study the formal garden, we should go first to the gardens of the Tuileries in Paris—an estate that had belonged to the royal family since the days of Francis I, who met and feasted with Henry VIII at the Field of Cloth of Gold.

Francis was considerably responsible for the introduction of the Italian Renaissance into France. And it was in the Renaissance manner that the Tuileries were to be developed by Catherine de Medici, after she became the widow of Henry II, successor to Francis.

They were made by Catherine de Medici formal in design: that is, they left no doubt in the minds of those who walked around them that they were designed and made by man for man—a display of the triumph of his art over the natural order. This was evident particularly in the use of water-cascades; ponds and fountains abounded—as in the Renaissance gardens of Italy; for in a country where water is scarce, the delight given by pools and the cool splash of fountains during summer may be imagined. The engineering of these waterworks, and particularly the construction of the conduits bringing the supplies often from far away, was an achievement requiring great skill.

But though water brought life to the gardens (it was often *l'âme du jardin*—the soul of the garden), their form was from a combination of regular features. Their pattern was geometrical, but as yet rather haphazard—as if many ingenious devices had been suddenly imagined and brought into being without relation to one another. Balustraded terraces, with widely sweeping stairways, were built where the fall of the ground made them possible. On level ground parterres were laid out. These were flower-beds shaped in the most fanciful patterns set among plots of mown grass or coloured gravels. The plants were in their turn placed to make patterns; the effect was something like embroidery on a green or gravelled ground. The parterres lay near the house. Beyond them radiated alleys and avenues leading to "bosquets". These were plantations of trees cut by paths laid in geometrical patterns—sometimes meeting in a lawn adorned with statues or fountains at the middle of the wood.

Arbours, tunnelled walks and pergolas were always a feature of these gardens. Sometimes they were shaped from living trees. Hornbeam and maple were used, and at the Tuileries an elaborate and much discussed design was once carried out in Italian cypress—which was all killed by the exceptionally severe winter of 1608. Often, however, "treillage" was used to form screens which divided one part of the garden from another. This was elaborate lattice-work held on stout pillars. The name, coming from "trellis"—vine tendrils—gives a hint of the complexity of design that was so skilfully developed.

Statuary—figures of mythical gods and goddesses, vases and urns—was placed at every possible point. It was spaced along terraces, ensconced in alcoves, and stood in the bosquets and elsewhere at the points where several paths intersected.

Then there were also what we can only call curiosities. Every great garden had its own maze or labyrinth. There was sure to be a grotto. Ideally, this was a mossy cave in a hillside, secreted and shaded by gnarled old trees. Statues of the appropriate Greek deities might stand sentinel at either side of the entrance. Inside, light flickered dimly on the walls, which glittered with elaborate patterns of shells, crystals and coloured tiles with which the walls were decorated. Even where there were neither hills nor caves, the most marvellous grottoes were contrived and built on the level ground.

There were orangeries too—substantial buildings pierced by rows of windows. Into them orange trees and other half-hardy shrubs, which stood out of doors in tubs or handsome vases during summer, were carried so that they might pass safely through the winter.

The pride of one garden was a quarry with a remarkable echo. In it parties were held to hear the trills of a famous singer thrown back without a fault.

Aviaries, all of the most beautiful design, filled with exotic birds, were sure to be found in some part of the garden, and as often as not a menagerie of wild animals in another.

One writer tells us of two great fish-ponds. Between these ponds there was a passageway of planks, in the cracks of which were a number of concealed brass jets. "While the ladies are amusing themselves with looking at the fish, those in the secret have only to touch a spring, which sets these jets in operation, and incontinently the petticoats and legs of the fair spectators are invaded with a refreshing coolness from these tiny water-spouts."

Those, then were the sort of features you would find in Italian Renaissance gardens that had become generally established on the great estates of France during the last half of the sixteenth century.

ANDRÉ LE NÔTRE

This was the kind of garden that the Tuileries had become when, on a spring day in 1613, probably in a little house within the gardens, a son was born to Jean Le Nôtre, Royal Master Gardener, who was in his turn son of Pierre Le Nôtre, Gardener-in-Chief of the Parterres of the Tuileries.

At the christening of the child with the name André he became still more involved in the gardening world, for his godmother was the wife of Claude Mollet, also of the third generation in a family of gardeners at that time even more famed than the Le Nôtres.

André was soon sent to learn the principles of architecture, painting and design. Having mastered the theories and principles of design, an apprenticeship followed in the Tuileries to learn the practical craft of gardening. All this time he lived with his father in the little house right inside the gardens; few men can have had finer opportunities to learn than he, and there is no doubt that he made the best of them. Apprenticeship ended, he was given a post, still within the Tuileries. Soon he married and in 1640 was appointed Designer in Ordinary of the King's Gardens.

During the first years of Louis XIV's reign Le Nôtre had clearly been progressing, for in 1657 he was made one of the three Controller-Generals of the Royal Buildings, and we can assume that his own share of the duties lay in taking charge of all the royal gardens.

But his real fame came to him first not as the royal gardener but as the designer of the gardens at Vaux-le-Vicomte for Nicolas Fouquet.

Fouquet was a financial genius who had attached himself to the Queen Mother's side after the death of Louis XIII. He became her superintendent of finance—a position which enabled him to amass a vast fortune for himself. This he spent lavishly on patronising the arts. He was, it seems, anxious to overawe and outshine the young Louis XIV, and began the building of a château at Vaux-le-Vicomte, designed to be the most magnificent that money could achieve. Le Vau was employed as the architect and Charles Le Brun as designer of all the furnishings. Le Brun had studied in Rome with the great Poussin and was a master of design. He was in addition a master of tact (largely directed to ensuring that his career should succeed) and a genius at organisation. It seems that he was responsible for the engagement of Le Nôtre as designer of the gardens for Fouquet.

In Vaux-le-Vicomte, Le Vau, Le Brun and Le Nôtre produced a triumph; a palace standing in a thousand acres of gardens and park. There was nothing to equal it in the whole of France. During its construction three hamlets disappeared, rivulets were diverted and whole woods transplanted.

When it was finished, Fouquet invited some six thousand people to a fête which would display all its glories (for the building also housed priceless collections of works of art and books). The King and the whole court were included. It is hard to imagine the grandeur of that August day in 1661, for its like has scarcely been repeated.

But we can imagine some of its drama.

All went outwardly well. The guests had a supper that cost over five thousand pounds. There were fireworks, illuminations, fountains arching into the sky, a play written specially for the occasion and directed by Molière himself . . .

Twenty days after the feast Fouquet was arrested; the rest of his life was spent in prison. Louis XIV was brooking no possible rival. The shady manner in which Fouquet had made his fortune was known to another of the King's ministers, Colbert—who succeeded to Fouquet's position. Fortunately, Colbert was as eager in his patronage of the arts and sciences as his predecessor had been.

The dramatic story of Vaux-le-Vicomte had, therefore, the happiest consequences for all concerned other than for the disgraced Fouquet.

First and foremost it seems to have determined Louis XIV to build at Versailles a palace that would be the most magnificent in all the world, transcending by far anything that his wealthiest subjects might attempt.

This in its turn set the pace and fashion for a wave of building that spread all over France and beyond. Le Vau, Le Brun and Le Nôtre achieved fame and unstinted opportunities to construct and design to their best ability regardless of expense.

We should consider what gave the gardens that he designed their special quality. He took all the parts that previously made up gardens—the fountains, parterres, bosquets, terraces and so on—and instead of arranging them in an almost haphazard manner, he composed them in one huge plan. Each part was fitted just where it looked best in the design, each played its part in the whole effect, none drew special attention to itself unless the master-mind of Le Nôtre thought: "Here we need something to catch the eye, something to stand out." Logic and reason and the classical ideals of regularity and symmetry, now brought into fashion, dominated the ingenuities and delights devised by the fertile minds of his predecessors.

Le Nôtre planned his gardens along a central axis; I have a picture of Vaux-le-Vicomte in front of me as I write. I can almost see Fouquet coming out of his great new house in the warm early morning sunshine of the fateful August day, taking one last look to make sure that all was well. There is the spot where he would stand on the paved terrace, at the head of the balustraded stairway which divides and curls down to the garden proper. He would see his garden stretching in one long vista, until it disappeared where the distant woods seemed to open slightly; a remote point, but with his garden equally divided on either side of a line as straight as a die stretching to it from where he stood. He saw this little nick between the distant woods directly over the broad path between the parterres that led to it, he saw it pointed precisely by the jet of the fountain that played high over a broad basin; beyond that, another spacious path still moved towards it, now with bosquets on either side. Still further the eye is carried along this relentless yet enchanting line, up to a distant narrowing glade, until at last it reaches to that dip in the trees which closes the vista, where the garden at last ends—or does it really end, or only disappear? Logic and reason allowed that final mystery.

And at right angles across the axis were laid other vistas, equally perfect, on a smaller scale. Within the bosquets, too, there were charming walks which disclosed themselves to the spectator as he moved from the house towards the distant woods; entering their shade, the statue of a nymph distantly seen would lead one along the path; then another hitherto undisclosed path would appear—a fountain playing into a circular basin at its end would draw you away from the nymph.

In other parts there were alleyways cut among the trees; elsewhere great double avenues of limes and beech and horsechestnut (the last a favourite of Le Nôtre) would everlastingly be leading the eye.

A feature of the gardens of Le Nôtre and his followers is that when you had been enticed up to some enchanting object, you would find that its design and workmanship were exquisite, and that the journey was not in vain. Le Nôtre excelled not only in his vast plans, but in the perfection of the detail; he was, too, a practical gardener and no doubt the plants were cultivated with a skill comparable with all else that he undertook.

Vaux-le-Vicomte was the first of his great gardens; with it he achieved fame and an almost unending series of commissions to design others. For some forty years he worked; his reputation and the influence of his theory of design spread far beyond France. Though he never visited England, there seems to be no doubt that he was to some extent concerned with the planning of the gardens at Greenwich and Hampton Court. Charles II, we recall, spent his exile with the French court and the knowledge of French arts and sciences that he and those who took refuge from the Commonwealth with him gained had an important effect on the progress of civilisation and culture in England.

It is, however, as designer of the royal gardens of Louis XIV that

Le Nôtre is best known. Soon after the fête at Vaux-le-Vicomte, Louis began to turn Versailles into a palace fit for the Sun King himself. The rest of the King's life was spent in the aggrandisement of France in the eyes of the world, and when not engaged in this, by concerning himself personally with a series of palaces, parks and gardens, all built with unexampled magnificence. In spite of the warnings of his ministers that his extravagances were imperilling his treasury, project followed project; no sooner did one seem complete than restlessly it was magnified, improved; none, it seems, were ever perfect in the eyes of this lavish builder.

Architects and designers fell out of favour—even the great Le Brun, who had become the dictator of the arts of France. But to the end Le Nôtre remained the designer of Louis' gardens—and a true friend of the King.

For the man was like his gardens—designed on the grand scale, honest, straightforward and balanced. When it came to the smaller details of his character, we still seem to see a parallel—however small, perfection was attempted, pettiness was avoided.

We meet him only in the writings and paintings of his friends, for he was far too busy to leave any record of his own life or work.

There is one painting of him made in middle age, when he had achieved success. Though he wears one of the long periwigs now come into fashion (it is said, to flatter Louis, the proud possessor of long and noble natural curls) and a robe-like garment, there is no hiding the strong character of a self-made man, one who has risen high but never despised his origins close to the soil. The long face is lively and intelligent, serious, but the shrewd, self-possessed dark eyes are ready to smile. It is the face, too, of a man who will gain his way happily, not by carping and criticising, but praising and even flattering.

When Charles II wrote to Louis XIV asking for Le Nôtre to be allowed to come and help with laying out the gardens at Greenwich, Louis wrote: "I have need of Le Nôtre continually"—a need that lasted until the old man retired from work.

Finally, we have in the accounts given by Dr. Martin Lister of his stay in Paris a delightful picture of Le Nôtre. He was then eighty-five, a "very ingenious" old gentleman, now almost a legend throughout Europe, a friend of the greatest men of the day. Wealthy, he could have lived in the grandest style, but Dr. Lister found him seated in his father's little house—now a garden-house—in the beloved Tuileries, surrounded by a collection of curios, medals and pictures.

His life and work is something of a fairy story. Did he, I wonder, as he sat there, find himself drifting into the world of Beauty and the Beast, of Mother Goose, of Puss in Boots? For his old friend the Controller of Gardens, Charles Perrault, was the author of these stories, and it was in the world of the gardens conceived in Le Nôtre's mind that we may place their setting.

A single garden remains in England where one can gain some understanding of the style of Le Nôtre. It is on a small scale, covering an area not comparable with the vast spaces often filled by the master, but the spirit that was the inspiration of his art is there.

In the south of Derbyshire, near the Leicestershire border, where the countryside is flat and a little uninteresting—quite the opposite of the romantic hills in the north of the county—lies the modern little industrial town of Melbourne, a town of no great fame. As you approach you turn away from the main road and within a few yards find yourself in a world quite remote from modern industry, the world of the old Melbourne that is famous in history as giving its name to Queen Victoria's Prime Minister, and to the city of Melbourne in Australia. By the side of the fine Norman church stands Melbourne Hall—by no means a grandiose building, and one that is the result of the accumulation of additions and alterations by the succeeding owners over hundreds of years.

A year or two after Le Nôtre's death, the owner of the Hall, Thomas Coke, who was Vice-Chamberlain to Queen Anne, employed Henry Wise to lay out the gardens. Henry Wise was born in Warwickshire in 1653, and led an active life as nurseryman, garden designer and gardener to William III, Queen Anne and George I. When he retired, he returned to his native county and died in 1738 at The Priory, Warwick (a building later removed wholesale to the United States of America). He was eminent, too, as a writer on gardening—his books being based on those of the French school.

At Melbourne, we know, he used Le Nôtre's Versailles to some extent as a model. By some good chance, Thomas Coke's garden was spared the tyrannical changes decreed by later fashions, and we can still see and feel something of the beauty and spirit of the style of gardening brought into being by the patronage of the unfortunate Fouquet and the over-resplendent Sun King.

I was there first on a thundery, showery day in July. At one moment all was dark and grey, the rain streaming down—at another the sun would be out in the glory of high summer. But as we were shown the house with its possessions, the rain poured down and it seemed that it would never cease. I was in the long room facing the gardens, listening attentively to our guide. Suddenly, a shaft of sunlight breaking through the storm caused me to look for the first time through the window at the gardens. The voice of the guide died away into the distance as my whole attention was drawn by the scene before me. Bright sun now shone on the drenched green garden, great dazzling storm clouds mounted the sky overhead. My eyes took in the view, followed the central vista, just as Henry Wise, more than two centuries ago, intended that they should. The first quick glance is drawn inevitably to the distant opening among the trees into which the garden disappeared. Then back I came to its beginning; to the terrace on which the windows opened. Urns mark its division from the sloping lawn across which a broad path leads boldly down the centre of the garden, its line made even more powerful by the emphasis of small trimmed bushes. On either side, spaced widely in the grass, stand low-branching catalpa trees, covered with their spikes of white foxglove flowers. Still descending, the path breaks its line momentarily to pass round a circular plot of grass, through whose centre the line is, however, remorselessly carried by narrow, erect trees. Then, its branches reunited, on goes the path, until it is brought to an abrupt stop by a large sheet of water. Dividing and passing on either side of this geometrically shaped pond, it meets again on the far side. The line of the axis is still maintained and marked now by taller, spiring trees. These are in themselves interesting for they are swamp cypresses—the same kind of tree about which we read earlier under which "proud Cortes" sat as he campaigned against the fabulous Montezuma. Then, beyond them the eye is caught by a silvery, metallic glitter. This, when you come up to it, is seen to be rather like a giant bird-cage elaborately fashioned in wrought-iron. By now the eye is set seeking among the distant trees and bosquets until it is led through a narrowing glade; at last, it seems, the garden disappears over the hill and far away.

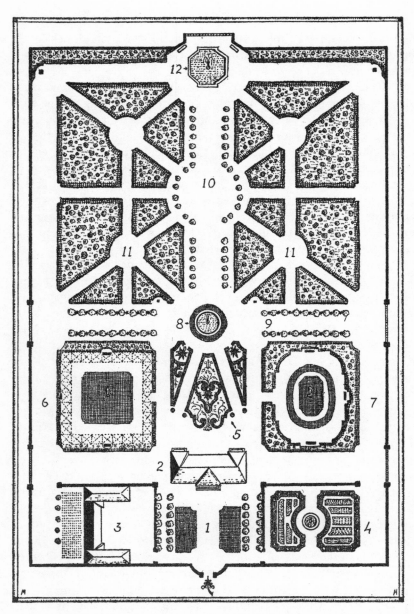

The plan of a formal garden at the end of the seventeenth century

A FORMAL GARDEN

Key

Approaching from a distance one sees the house and garden enclosed entirely between high walls, here and there broken by small gaps or grills, filled with open ironwork. Within the gates is a courtyard (1) immediately in front of the house (2). On either side are plots of grass in front of treed alleys, beyond which are walls. Behind the wall on the left rise the roofs of the stables and outbuildings (3), which hide a nursery garden. Balancing this on the right is the neatly laid-out kitchen garden (4), with a small fountain at its centre. From the window of a room overlooking the garden one has a view uninterruptedly along the broad central axis to the water at its far end; beyond that, through a grill opening in the wall, there is a narrowed view of the country beyond. In the foreground is a decorative parterre (5). From it one enters on the left a "green hall" (6), with a bowling green inside; to its right is an oval walk surrounded and hidden by shrubs (7). Two paths through the parterre converge on a fountain playing over a circular basin rimmed with green turf (8). This is a vantage point. From it one looks left and right along broad alleys (9) lined with horse-chestnuts and yews planted alternately; looking up them the country can be seen through the grills. Straight ahead is the main alley (10), with fine trees; at an angle both left and right are paths leading into the recesses of woods or bosquets (11), beyond which is the great basin (12) with its fountains.

I have made a drawing from a plan that I found in an old gardening book of Queen Anne's day—one, incidentally, to which Coke of Melbourne was a subscriber. Though this is a small garden, of a type fit only "for the houses of private persons", it will give some idea of a garden in the style of Le Nôtre.

CHAPTER 4

Botanic Gardeners

It is often difficult to find the dividing line between pioneers in gardening, who interest us in this book, and pioneers of botany, who do not. But botanic gardens, particularly the early ones, are, I think, part of the story. In them were developed the skill and craft necessary to grow those plants difficult in cultivation. So some, at least, of those responsible for the management of the first botanists' gardens must have a place here.

The earliest of these gardens were concerned only with cultivating those plants which the doctors of the day thought were useful in healing maladies. Such gardens existed in Italy during the fourteenth century. Gradually more interest was taken in the study of the plants themselves, though their use by apothecaries and herbalists as "simples" was still the urge that lay behind their study.

The honour of making the first real botanic garden goes to the ancient city of Padua, not far from Venice. The place was already famed for its university established in the Middle Ages, which was a pioneer in the study of natural history. Then, to provide specimens for the study of plants, one Bonafede pointed out the need for a public garden in which they might be cultivated specially for this purpose. The growth and study of exotic plants (that is, those growing only outside Italy) was to be a special feature. Bonafede put forward his plan in 1543, and the garden was soon brought into being. Thus began a long history which continued down to this day—though in the eighteenth century the purpose of the garden became solely botanical and no longer medical. Yet, even in its early days, a great many plants were grown and studied there which were scarcely of medicinal value. At that period the merchants of Venice were sailing all over the world, and Padua was probably the first garden in the world to send out collectors, who travelled on the Venetian ships for the sole purpose of bringing back new plants to the "Orto Botanico", as it was called.

The names of the directors and gardeners are now largely forgotten, but the result of their work remains. For instance, through Padua some of the earliest hyacinths were introduced to Europe, as well as some of the first tulips to be seen here.

Padua also claims the first plane tree to be grown in Europe, a tree still standing, and planted in 1670. The same claim is made for an American Bullbay—the giant evergreen magnolia often grown against the walls of houses in this country. This was planted in 1750. The oldest plant in the garden is a shrub, oddly called the Chaste Tree, which was there in 1550 and so must have been quite a good-sized youngster when Queen Elizabeth I came to the throne.

In the following years botanic gardens were made at several of the other old university towns of Europe. In 1597, for instance, was established what later became the Jardin des Plantes, the important botanical garden at Paris—though its original purpose was to supply flowers for making up the bouquets used at the royal court.

Montpellier, in the south of France, was another of the old university towns to be in the van with the establishment of a botanic garden. This was largely due to the energy of one man, Pierre Richer de Belleval. He claimed that his students were leaving Montpellier for those Italian universities such as Padua which had gardens where living plants could be studied, and urged that his own university should have a similar place. He won his point, and in 1596 the King of France gave instructions for land to be acquired and a gardener to be paid. With this royal support, the garden was soon in being.

It is interesting to compare Belleval's ideas of a garden with that at Padua. The Italian garden was circular in shape, secluded within a high wall. There were two main paths, each straight and at right angles to one another, converging on a central fountain. Four handsome gateways in the wall terminated each path. Within the wall, the garden was laid out in a geometrical pattern. Four square beds filled most of the circle, each divided into 125 small, numbered compartments to hold the plants. These beds were surrounded by a wide path, with another wide rim of small beds against the inside of the circular wall. Outside the wall, trees were planted. The garden stood surrounded by the beautiful buildings of Padua, and as geometrical in design as it could possibly be; the only irregularities came from the forms of the plants and occasional trees.

Belleval's ideas for Montpellier were quite different. Perhaps because he had studied and drawn hundreds of wild plants in their homes, he constructed a large mound, with beds in terraces. In these he tried to place the plants as they grew in nature. Those from high mountains he planted at the top (was his the first rock-garden?). Then lower down the slopes came the trees and plants from wooded hills. Finally, on one side of the mound he made an artificial marsh where aquatic plants were grown. This was an interesting development in gardening—a pioneer example of a feature in many present-day gardens. The medicinal plants were grown in an orderly plot on their own, while a patch of meadowland in which the native wild flowers could be studied as they grew naturally was carefully retained. In addition, there were other features such as damp, shady rockeries and grottos, where ferns and mosses thrived.

Belleval was a clever and successful gardener. Within a few years he had happily established over one thousand three hundred different kinds of plants. He introduced the mulberry tree to the gardens, and from thence to the surrounding districts, where its cultivation soon brought in much wealth. Plants were collected from the not far distant mountains—Cevennes, Alps and Pyrenees—another original experiment.

Then unfortunately civil war broke out between Huguenots and Catholics. In 1622, when Montpellier was heavily fortified, Belleval's garden was in the ring of the outer defences. Within a few days his mound was demolished and thirty years' work undone. Some of the rarest plants were hurriedly moved to another garden, but winter had set in and most of them died. Belleval himself became an army surgeon, and no doubt made valuable use of his great knowledge of medicinal plants.

When peace was restored the Montpellier gardens were replanted. At one time or another some of the world's most famous botanists taught or learned there—but as none combined as he had the qualities of pioneer and gardener, we need not name others.

Not only those gardens that we have described, but half a dozen others on the continent of Europe had been famous for a number of years when, on the afternoon of St. James's Day, 1621, with much pomp, ceremony and speech-making, Oxford University Botanic Garden was opened. This garden, which can still be visited was the first to be established in the British Isles.

We read that Henry, Lord Danvers, "being minded to become a benefactor to the University, determined to begin and finish a place whereby learning, especially the faculty of medicine, might be improved." To do this, he decided to found a garden like those he had no doubt seen while on his foreign travels. He set about the job, succeeded in getting a suitable site, and was the moving spirit in bringing this first garden into being.

Danvers was a picturesque character. As a boy, he had been page to that most wise and gallant statesman, poet and soldier Sir Philip Sidney (he may even have been with him at Zutphen). He travelled much, and spent some time in France, outlawed from England under suspicion of murder. We may remember him each time we enter the gardens through the lovely old gateway built by Nicholas Stone at his expense.

The first head gardener was a foreigner, Jacob Bobart, from Brunswick. He lives on in the history of the University as one of Oxford's oddest characters. A swarthy-looking man, he wore a long black beard dropping to his waist, and on the occasions of University celebrations, he tagged this out with pieces of silver. When walking about, a goat followed at his heels instead of the usual dog.

However odd his appearance, he was a very fine gardener. By 1648, when he compiled a catalogue of the gardens, his collection of plants consisted of some sixteen hundred different species and varieties. There was, for instance, what we should even now call a remarkable collection of primulas. Some of them are rarities to this day, difficult to grow and hard to come by. Bobart describes them so: "Feild Cowslips, Feild Oxelips, Double Paigles, Cowslips two in a hose, Feild Primerose, Double White Primerose, Single Blew Primerose, Green Primerose and Curl'd Cowslip." Bearing in mind that a double paigle is a double cowslip, how many of these primulas can you find in gardens today? If you start searching, I think you will realise that old Jacob had not only collected some great rarities, but was a skilful gardener to keep them happy in his garden.

While Bobart was the gardener, Dr. Robert Morison was the first University professor of botany. A physician who came from Aberdeen, he made valuable use of the Oxford gardens in one of the first attempts to classify plants according to a system. This was an important work, finished after his death in 1683 by the son of old Jacob Bobart. Also a Jacob, Bobart the younger succeeded Morison as professor. Like his father, he was a peculiar man—dirty, untidy and of evil appearance. With a glance at him through the eyes of a visiting German we may leave the pioneers at Oxford: "Such was the aspect of the Herr Professor that no one would have taken him for anything but a gardener."

In 1673 the second English botanical garden was established. In that year the London Apothecaries Company, that body of men who kept what today would be rather like chemists' shops, leased a plot of land at Chelsea. Here they hoped to grow and study the herbs and plants—particularly some of the new ones coming from abroad—that they used for healing.

At that time Chelsea was a pleasant village surrounded by fields, the smoke from distant London for much of the year being blown away from it by the prevailing south and west winds. The Company wanted a riverside site so that they might travel to their garden from the City by barge up the River Thames, then London's main highway. Suitable land was leased from Charles Cheyne—and the remains of "Physick Garden", as it was called, still exist not far from Cheyne Walk, which commemorates the name of the Company's first landlord.

By 1674 the site was enclosed in a high wall. By 1685, under the Keeper, Mr. Watts, much progress had been made, as is recorded by John Evelyn in his diary: "There is a collection of innumerable rarities . . . many rare annuals, the tree bearing Jesuit's bark* which had done such wonders in agues. What was very ingenious was the subterranean

---

* The early name for quinine.

heat, conveyed by a stove under the conservatory, all vaulted with brick, so as the doors and windows are open in the hardest frost."

The garden was, however, not altogether successful. One of the troubles was the distance that lay between Chelsea and the Company's quarters in the City.

Early in the next century things got better. The most eminent and successful physician of the age, Sir Hans Sloane (the first doctor ever to be made a baronet), invested some of his riches by acquiring the Manor of Chelsea. He was deeply interested in the sciences, particularly botany. In 1722 he allowed the Apothecaries Company the use of the land on which their garden stood at a very low rent, but at the same time laying down conditions which ensured that the garden was properly run.

Philip Miller comes into the story at this point. He was born near London, the son of a Scotsman. Trained as a gardener, he eventually set up as a "florist" (or nurseryman, we should now call him) on land at St. George's Fields on which the King's Bench Prison was later built. Here Sir Hans Sloane got to know him, and was impressed not only with his skill as a gardener, but with his exceptional knowledge of the botanical features of the plants under his care. It was probably through Sloane's influence with the Apothecaries Company that in 1722 Miller was made head gardener at Chelsea. The director at the time was a certain Isaac Rand—a learned but hot-tempered and difficult man, whose reputation was soon quite eclipsed by the fame of his gardener, for in 1724 was issued the first volume of Philip Miller's *The Gardeners' Dictionary*. When completed, this work long held the stage as the standard English dictionary of gardening. In it Miller combined his wide practical knowledge of plants and their cultivation with a sound understanding of botany. It was well written and easily understood. Its fame soon spread far beyond Britain. Miller's names and descriptions of some plants included in his dictionary are still used by botanists. At Chelsea his zeal and enthusiasm soon transformed the garden and brought it into a leading place. Many instances are recorded of his skill—how he germinated seeds that no one else could grow by placing them on a bed of tan, which becomes slightly heated, and how he was the first to flower bulbs by standing them in narrow-necked glasses of water. He was also one of the first to draw attention to the important part that insects play in transferring pollen from the anthers to the styles of flowers.

Philip Miller, as may be imagined, was a strong and energetic character, not well able to tolerate those whom he considered foolish. A dislike of the Scots still lingered on among Englishmen, and although born in London, he was considered "one of those northern lads who have invaded the southern provinces". There are, therefore, quite a number of tales told of his meanness and secrecy. But the fact seems to be that to those he considered worthy, he was most generous in gifts of rare plants, help and valuable advice founded on his wide experience.

Many famous gardeners and botanists came to Chelsea both to see the plants and talk with the head gardener. One of the most important meetings in the Apothecaries Garden was between Miller and Linnaeus.

Carolus Linnaeus, or Carl von Linné as he afterwards became, was a botanist. His importance is due to his work in classifying plants and inventing a system of naming them which has been of much help to gardeners.

Linnaeus was born in 1707, in the south of Sweden, where his father Nils was pastor of a small parish.

When asked to account for his tenacious memory, Carolus used to tell how, when a small boy, he was continually asking questions about plants. Sometimes he asked a question a second time, having forgotten the answer. His father, no doubt rather wearied by the endless curiosity of his son, threatened never to answer again a question that he had already answered. The boy took the hint, and made sure that anything once explained was never forgotten.

Linnaeus was, his family hoped, to follow his father's footsteps in the church. The family were not well off, and sacrifices were made so that the boy might have the necessary education. How unhappy the old pastor must have been when he learned that his son, though of excellent character, was no good at his lessons and was held to be more suitable for apprenticeship as a tailor or shoemaker than for the church!

At this time Nils Linnaeus went to consult his doctor, a friend of the family, about some illness from which he suffered. The old man told his doctor the sad news about the dullness of his boy. But it seems the doctor knew something of the youngster and grasped what was wrong. Carolus was clever enough, but quite uninterested in theology and the other subjects he had to study in order to enter the church. The doctor offered to take him into his own home during the year that must be spent at school if he was to go on to a university. At the same time he coached him privately in physiology and taught him how to go about the study of plants. In the next examinations concerned with these subjects Linnaeus distinguished himself.

The years that followed were difficult. Natural history—a subject of which Linnaeus was laboriously acquiring such a complete mastery—was still of little account in the world of learning. Always hard up, he moved from job to job, and was at times dependent on patrons who realised his true worth. He travelled widely. He was not, it seems, easy to get on with: possession of a knowledge so much wider than that of most of the professors of the day often resulted in bitterness and feuds. (He had to leave Hamburg hurriedly after demonstrating that a seven-headed hydra was a fake—so great was the feeling aroused against him by this exposure of a legend.)

He also made important journeys of exploration, visiting Lapland and suffering many privations. His published works on the classification of plants brought him fame on the continent of Europe where he had spent much time, and he returned to Stockholm with a view to marrying and settling down as a physician.

Unhappily his reputation had not yet reached his native country, and he was to suffer more difficult years before he built up a practice. At last he was appointed to a professorship at Upsala University and his life became one of continuing prosperity and fame. In 1761 he was raised to the nobility, and from the humble Carolus Linnaeus who couldn't pass his exams became the distinguished Professor Carl von Linné of the University of Upsala.

Linnaeus might have qualified as a pioneer on account of his many studies of differing aspects of natural history, or from his important accounts of the plants of little-known places. He might stake a claim as the deviser of the first practicable system of classifying plants—though this has been superseded since. But it is as the inventor of the system of naming living things—animals, birds and plants—that we all particularly pay tribute to Linnaeus, gardeners no less than scientists.

From early days, European scientists used the Latin language for their writings. This was an international tongue used by all learned people. A German could therefore understand a treatise written by an Italian, though the two men might be unable to speak each other's daily language. Plants were recognised among botanists by names which amounted to a short Latin description. For example, Parkinson called rhubarb *Hippolopathum maximum rotundifolium exoticum*, and even Belleval of Montpellier named a toadflax *Linaria anthochrysosocyandrepis*! It was all bewildering and confusing.

As we have seen, the work of Linnaeus was largely concerned with classification of plants. His keen memory and powerful eyesight aided him in his first step, drawing up accurate descriptions. Comparing these with those made in the past by his predecessors, he would often find that one and the same plant might carry several distinct names, each one given to it by a different authority. In addition long names were in practice unwieldy and laborious to use.

In his system of classification of plants, Linnaeus went carefully through his detailed descriptions and then grouped together those plants that he found to have flowers of similar construction. The most important groups or units were called the *genera* and within the genus came a division into *species*.

From these two units Linnaeus evolved his new method of nomenclature. First comes the name of the genus into which it is put, then a specific name or "epithet" which distinguishes it from the other species within the genus. The whole paraphernalia of long-winded names collapses, and a simple and universal system using two names only for identifying every plant takes its place.

It is perhaps necessary to add that with the development of science, the Linnaean system of classification has been amended and his so-called "binomial" method of naming developed rather further to include sub-species and varieties, but the underlying principles, so simple as to be typical of a genius, remain.

The names of many genera are adaptations of the old classical names of plants. *Castanea*, the genus containing the chestnuts, is the Latin name for the sweet chestnut. Others describe the plant in some way, such as *Helianthus*, which combines the Greek words "sun" and "flower"—an obvious and appropriate name for the genus including sunflowers. A good many of those genera not known to the ancients are given names commemorating famous botanists. Linnaeus was very apt at choosing appropriate names. He dedicated *Magnolia* to Pierre Magnol (who was a native of Montpellier), because "it is handsome both in foliage and flower and worthy of so fine a man." The director of the Chelsea gardens under whom Miller first worked is commemorated by *Randia*, a genus of tropical and often thorny plants, and the story is that Linnaeus chose the name on account of Isaac Rand's hot temper and prickly nature.

The specific names or epithets are similarly chosen, though more usually they are descriptive. We have *Castanea sativa*, the sweet chestnut, long grown on the Continent for its fruit, *sativa* meaning cultivated. Or again, *Magnolia grandiflora*, the well-named large-flowered magnolia.

Parkinson's long-winded name for our common rhubarb disappeared, and Linnaeus replaced it with *Rheum rhaponticum*. *Rheum*, the name of the genus, is evolved from an old name for medicinal rhubarb; *rhaponticum*, the name of the species, means that kind of rhubarb found growing in the district of the Black Sea.

Today we can see the virtue of this simplicity compared with the cumbersome old methods of classification and naming of plants. We are not surprised to learn that the views of Linnaeus, so revolutionary, upset those who had become thoroughly embedded in the old ways. Matters were not made easier by Linnaeus himself, who though quite rightly self-confident in the merits of his new system, took few pains to be tactful when putting his views before his older colleagues. Such was Philip Miller who certainly formed the opinion that the younger man was merely a conceited upstart.

To Linnaeus it was apparent that England now had two highly important centres of botanical and horticultural learning—the Oxford Botanic Gardens and Miller's Chelsea Garden. So in 1736 he came here to see both at first hand.

The meeting of these two men in the old Apothecaries' Garden by the Thames was an awkward affair. Miller received Linnaeus as if he were a junior of little consequence. His opinion was confirmed after they had walked round the collection of plants. Linnaeus did little more than ask the names of plants, which Miller rolled off learnedly in the long-winded old-fashioned style. Miller was now quite sure that the young man from Sweden who was making such a stir on the Continent was an upstart, and a very ignorant one at that; why else would he have asked so many simple questions?

Later the two of them made the rounds of the garden again. This time Linnaeus led Miller, and instead of asking the names, he now told him what they were—but now according to his new, simplified system.

This meeting might be considered an unhappy event. By it, however, Linnaeus was confirmed in his view that Miller, awkward though he seemed, was a wise and capable man of clear intellect. And happily this proved to be true. Miller soon began to think over all the things that the young Swede had said and which at the time annoyed him so strongly. He realised that Linnaeus was after all on the right lines. In the battle that followed over the general introduction of the Linnaean systems, Miller was their strong champion, and the great *Gardeners' Dictionary* was altered to accord with it.

Linnaeus, for his part, gratefully acknowledged the help that Miller gave him in later years.

Miller has another claim to fame. In 1732 he collected seed of the cotton plant grown in the garden. This he sent to the young American colony of Georgia, and from it young plants were successfully raised. From them much of the cotton now grown in the United States of America is descended.

After forty-eight years spent in the Apothecaries' Garden, always underpaid and often in disagreement with his employers, the old man was pensioned off in 1770. The year after, he died aged eighty. Sir Hans Sloane's recommendation of nearly half a century before was abundantly justified; the Chelsea Apothecaries' Garden during that period had been famed throughout the world. Not the least important feature of his reign was his training of men who carried on his high traditions long after he had gone. Miller himself was succeeded by one of them, William Forsyth. But he belongs to another chapter.

The reputation of the Apothecaries' Garden declined later and neglect followed, until the end of the last century, when it was put in order again and taken over for the use of certain London colleges. It was thenceforward an entirely scientific institution, which it still is. Several ancient trees and shrubs remain as relics of the past, but they can only be seen by students, for the garden is not open to the public.

So many of the pioneers in gardening are men who have left Scotland that it may be as well to record some of those who stayed and worked in their own country. One of these was Robert Sibbald. In 1661 he returned from Holland, where he learned the practice of medicine, to Edinburgh. There was at that time no medical school at the University; the standard of practice was therefore dreadfully low. Horrified by the ignorance of the "quack" apothecaries and surgeons compared with their fellows in more enlightened Continental cities, Sibbald determined to improve matters in his own country. In the year 1670, therefore, he purchased land on which to grow medicinal plants in order to demonstrate their uses. Helped by a youth named James Sutherland, a collection of a thousand plants was soon got together.

Sir Robert Sibbald, as he later became, was a many-sided man. Not only was he the first professor of medicine at Edinburgh University, but also Geographer-Royal and a writer on antiquarian matters.

Sutherland, an enthusiast for plants from his childhood days, was later appointed professor of botany in the University, and, by William III, King's Botanist. It was almost certainly he who planted the great yew in the present Edinburgh Royal Botanic gardens, which has been twice transplanted when the garden was moved. In 1683 he published a catalogue of about two thousand plants growing in the garden, among them one of the first larch trees recorded in Britain.

The Edinburgh garden stands among the first three botanic gardens to be made within the British Isles. Its greatest claim to fame as a pioneer in gardening, however, did not come until some two hundred years later. Towards the end of the last century, under the Keepership of Sir Isaac Bayley Balfour, the situation was found to suit the hundreds of new plants—alpines, primulas, gentians, lilies and particularly rhododendrons—then being sent from China. Under Sir Isaac one of the most remarkable rock-gardens in the world was built. Edinburgh remains, too, one of the chief centres concerned with the study of the vast genus of rhododendrons, so many of which have been introduced into this country during the present century.

CHAPTER 5

Garden Into Landscape

The last garden we described was at Melbourne—a garden in which compasses, dividers and rulers mastered nature. Later this fashion of formality became even more overpowering. Avenues were all the rage—straight as a die (Lord Montagu planted seventy-three miles of them, all radiating from his house in Northamptonshire). Hedges were cut into more and more fantastic shapes. Indeed, the formal garden, lovely though it might be, was becoming too formal—at times resulting in a comic monstrosity.

Fashion, as usual, was bound to change and the pendulum to swing the other way. The men who lifted the weight back so that it might gain momentum for a new sweep were not gardeners or craftsmen, but writers—literary men. Books and paintings brought "nature" in one of her many guises back into the garden.

In the *Spectator* of September 1712 one may read:

> "I am one, you must know, who am looked upon as an humorist in gardening. I have several acres about my house, which I call my garden, and which a skilful gardener would not know what to call. It is a confusion of kitchen and parterre, orchard and flower-garden, which lie so mixed and interwoven with one another, that if a foreigner who had seen nothing of our country should be conveyed into

my garden at his first landing, he would look upon it as a natural wilderness, and one of the uncultivated parts of our country. My flowers grow up in several parts of the garden in the greatest luxuriancy and profusion. I am so far from being fond of any particular one, by reason of its rarity, that if I meet with any one in a field which pleases me, I give it a place in my garden. By this means, when a stranger walks with me, he is surprised to see several large spots of ground covered with ten thousand different colours, and has often singled out flowers that he might have met with under a common hedge, in a field, or in a meadow, as some of the greatest beauties of the place. The only method I observe in this particular, is to range in the same quarter the products of the same season, that they may make their appearance together, and compose a picture of the greatest variety. There is the same irregularity in my plantations, which run into as great a wildness as their natures will permit. I take in none that do not naturally rejoice in the soil, and am pleased, when I am walking in a labyrinth of my own raising, not to know whether the next tree I shall meet with is an apple or an oak, an elm or a pear-tree. My kitchen has likewise its particular quarters assigned it; for besides the wholesome luxury which that place abounds with, I have always thought a kitchen-garden a more pleasant sight than the finest orangery or artificial green-house. I love to see everything in its perfection, and am more pleased to survey my coleworts and cabbages, with a thousand nameless pot-herbs, springing up in their full fragrancy and verdure, than to see the tender plants of foreign countries kept alive by artificial heats, or withering in an air or soil that are not adapted to them. I must not omit, that there is a fountain rising in the upper part of my garden, which forms a little wandering rill, and administers to the pleasure as well as the plenty of the place. I have so conducted it, that it visits most of my plantations; and have taken particular care to let it run in the same manner as it would do in an open field, so that it generally passes through banks of violets and primroses, plats of willow, or other plants, that seem to be of its own producing. There is

another circumstance in which I am very particular, or, as my
neighbours call me, very whimsical: as my garden invites into
it the birds of the country, by offering them the conveniency
of springs and shades, solitude and shelter, I do not suffer any
one to destroy their nests in the spring, or drive them from their
usual haunts in fruit-time. I value my garden more for being
full of blackbirds than cherries, and very frankly give them
fruit for their songs. By this means I have always the music
of the season in its perfection, and am highly delighted to see
the jay or the thrush hopping about my walks, and shooting
before my eye across the several little glades and alleys that I
pass through."

That was during Queen Anne's reign, and it expressed a taste which
slowly became current. Pope and all his friends supported it. To be
a man of taste—and in George II's reign every man of consequence
aspired to be this as a matter of national pride—one had to get busy,
cut down hedges, dig up parterres and let nature come into the garden.
Again the fashion was being set, not by gardeners, but by poets and
journalists.

"The humorist in gardening", for instance, was Joseph Addison. The
old-fashioned gardener with his skill and love of plants was the butt of
these writers. There was the famous "catalogue of greens to be disposed
of by an eminent gardener" which satirised the elaborately clipped evergreens produced by the skilled craftsman which had become so popular:

"Adam and Eve in holly; Adam a little shattered by the fall of
the tree of Knowledge in the great storm; Eve and the serpent
very flourishing.
    Noah's Ark in holly, the ribs a little damaged for want
of water.
    The Tower of Babel not yet finished.
    St. George in box; his arm scarce long enough, but will be
in a condition to stick the dragon by next April.
    A green dragon of the same, with a tail of ground ivy for
the present.
    N.B. These two are not to be sold separately."

And so on.

To counter these assaults by the literary gentlemen, the gardeners had had to alter their style somewhat. Even Henry Wise, the disciple of Le Nôtre, introduced more freedom in his last designs. The first of the important professional gardeners to yield to the world of literature was, however, Charles Bridgeman. We do not know much about him. He died in 1738, having been Royal Gardener for eighteen years, and was one of the few gardeners who received the approval of the poetic dictator of English taste, Alexander Pope. Indeed, Bridgeman helped the poet to build a grotto in his famous garden at Twickenham.

Yet there was much of the old style of garden in Bridgeman's design: it was written of him that "he disdained to make every division tally with its opposite, and though he still adhered much to straight walks with high clipped hedges, the rest he diversified by wilderness and with loose groves of oak".

At last the formal garden disappeared, and was replaced by a scene that

> . . . scoops in circling theatres the vale,
> Calls in the country, catches opening glades,
> Joins willing woods, and varies shades from shades.

It was a scene, too, which plainly showed that its designer had thrown away his ruler and compasses; and laws of mathematic proportions were abolished and replaced by one rule only:

"Let Nature never be forgot."

WILLIAM KENT

Kent was a rather poor painter, a fine architect, a genius at interior decoration and designing furniture, state carriages, royal barges and the like—practically everything except a gardener.

Few men were more able to grasp the opportunities that came. He was born in 1684 of obscure parents at Bridlington, in Yorkshire; all his life he showed the qualities associated with men from that county. As a youth he is supposed to have been apprenticed to a coachpainter. Ambitious to be a famous painter, he went to Rome, at that time the centre of the European world of art. Here he was under the patronage of a certain Burrell Massingberd, squire of Ormsby in Lincolnshire. This Massingberd was typical of a certain class of the English nobility and gentry of the day. To him, the grand tour of Europe was an essential part of education—the final stage. A study of the arts in Italy was necessary to put the finishing touches to this tour; and Massingberd, as was not unusual, stayed on and made a more protracted visit to pursue his education more thoroughly. As we can still often see when visiting old houses, he and his like collected Italian paintings to bring home, and also employed artists to work for them in the Italian manner, or to make copies of those Italian paintings which they admired but were unable to bring away. So great was the fashion for Italian art, and such an important centre of the art world was Italy, that any ambitious young English artist tried to make his way out there, develop his style of painting in the correct Italian manner, and secure patronage from the visiting gentry. Such an artist was Kent, and Massingberd was the patron who took him under his wing, and who no doubt introduced him into the circle of nobility and gentry then centred on Rome.

Yorkshire energy and good companionship seem to have done the rest. The young artist, while always good and cheerful company, was devoid of that obsequiousness shown by many of his fellows towards their rich patrons. He had his own decided opinions, too, held them firmly, and was not too indiscreet in expressing them. His parts were such that he soon became of some account in the cosmopolitan society of Rome, moving freely among the visiting aristocracy. His character and popularity no doubt accounted for an exaggerated opinion of his skill as a painter; he won several prizes, and was even hailed as a "second Raphael"—all quite unmerited.

One of the important visitors to Rome at that time was the youthful Richard Boyle, Earl of Burlington and Cork, vastly rich, with big estates in Yorkshire. He had inherited his titles and lands as a boy, and took his responsibilities seriously. He was an exceptionally talented young man and had lately become absorbed in the study of architecture—studies which were later to have a strong influence on English building.

Perhaps it was Yorkshire fellowship that first drew Lord Burlington to William Kent. For not only was he to become Kent's patron, but a lifelong friend. In 1719 he brought him back from Rome and installed him at Burlington House in London, where he lived, a member of the household. The friendship and partnership of the two men remained close until Kent's death.

Impelled by the driving force and strongly held theories of Burlington, the two took to architecture. Kent practically ceased to paint, and henceforth devoted himself to the propagation and practice of his patron's views. These produced what is called the Palladian school of architecture, a movement which dominated fashionable building design for a considerable period and is intimately connected with the English garden. The architectural aspect of Kent's work does not concern us, interesting and delightful though it is; the extraordinary change that, almost as a sideline, he effected in our gardens is the matter we have to discuss.

His first garden design, which has all the elements of his later work, was for the house (a famous one in the history of architecture) that Lord Burlington designed for himself at Chiswick. But for the most part Kent "improved", or added to, existing gardens. This he did by throwing down the walls or hedges that enclosed them, and making them part of the surrounding landscape into which they merged. In their place, he cut a special type of ditch. This effectively stopped cattle and horses entering the garden proper but was invisible from a short distance. To those walking round the garden for the first time, it seemed that it was unconfined, stretching to the distant wood or curling lake-side; then, as the unsuspecting visitor reached the ditch that protected the house and garden from the beasts of the field, Ha! Ha! he exclaimed. And so these ditches have been given the name of ha-has. The invention, oddly enough, was a French one used at the end of long formal alleyways to provide a "claire-voie" or "clear view" into the surrounding country. It was a narrow view only, however. Kent, improving on Bridgeman's practice, used it to such an extent that all the garden began to seem part of the countryside. To complete the illusion, the orchards and kitchen-garden and the plots in which the few flowers grew were moved far away from the house; here they were grown in a walled garden, discreetly embowered and hidden among trees. The

humdrum vegetable and fruit-growing part of gardening had nothing
to do with "nature" as she was now understood, and had to be tucked
away out of sight!

And what exactly did William Kent, Lord Burlington, Alexander
Pope and all the rest of them mean by "nature"?

One may get a good idea by going into the nearest art gallery and
finding a landscape by Salvator Rosa or Claude. They are not much like
"nature" as we understand it. They were idealised, imagined landscapes
in which the romantic beauties of "nature"—hills, dales, woods, lawns,
splashing cataracts and glassy mirror-like lakes played their part as on
a stage. Works of man were to be found in the scene too: they were
placed at some point to which the eye of the beholders was led. These
buildings were always ancient—perhaps a mediaeval ruin or a Roman
temple, something which the mind of an educated man could associate
with some anecdote of past times.

The different parts of this landscape led gently one into another by
sinuous curves, (curves that are so fortunately found in the gentle hills
of much of England). The straight line was forbidden; never again was
an avenue to be planted, and many were, unhappily, felled as contrary
to "nature".

William Kent's most famous and loudly acclaimed triumph was at
Stowe in Buckinghamshire. This place had become the home of Sir
Richard Temple, a soldier with a distinguished gallant record who
had served under Marlborough and was created Viscount Cobham. In
the year 1713 he began to alter his garden—and, in fact, being a true
gardener, he never ceased doing so during the rest of his life. He was
an admirer of the new school. First Bridgeman was called in, and broke
down some of the formality of the old garden; and Sir John Vanbrugh
added some ornamental buildings. Then Kent was called in. It was here
that he "jumped the fence"—or rather, took it down and replaced it by
his ha-has—on the grand scale. Vistas were arranged in every direction.
Each one ended in a temple, a ruin, a bridge or a hermitage. Some, of
course, were the work of Vanbrugh, but most of them delightful little
conceits designed by Kent. They were dedicated "to every conceivable
deity and virtue"; there were no less than thirty-eight, so many that a
French writer said that "My Lord Temple has been too much led astray
by his name"! These buildings were skilfully placed in glades newly

Cross-section of a ha-ha

cut or planted. Where water was used, instead of being trained into canal-like streams and spouting from massive fountains, it now trickled "naturally" from springs (most ingeniously and artificially devised, it is true) and wound its way "naturally" in serpentine curves carefully contrived by Kent. A pool, designed in the shape of an octagon and constructed with no little difficulty by his predecessors, had its regular margins broken up and "naturalised".

Stowe Gardens now became famous; all persons of note duly paid their visits of inspection. Cobham and Kent became the acknowledged leaders of the new school of gardening.

Yet Stowe and most of Kent's other gardens were no more than "improvements"—and revolutionary at that—of existing gardens. They set an example which was followed by many landowners who prided themselves on being men of taste and fashion. Such a one was Sir Thomas Lyttleton, of Hagley in Worcestershire. Like Cobham he was a friend of Alexander Pope. Having absorbed all the new ideas of gardening and with the example of Stowe and other similar work before him, he set about transforming his own estate, ideally situated for the purpose among the little hills of Worcestershire, into an "Elysium" in the new manner. Unlike Lord Cobham, he was unhampered by any existing garden on the grand scale. Today we can still see much of Lyttleton's "landscape gardening". (This term, which at first described the kind of garden that William Kent brought into being, was invented by Lyttleton's neighbour, the poet William Shenstone, who laid out a similar kind of garden at the Leasowes on a smaller scale.) Yet, to gain a proper idea of what it meant to Lyttleton and his friends, we should, I think, turn to a description of Hagley written when the style of Kent could still be called that of "modern gardening".

> "The house, though low in the park, is yet above the adjacent country, which it overlooks to a very distant horizon: it is surrounded by a lawn of fine uneven ground, and diversified with large clumps, little groupes, and single trees; it is open in front, but covered on one side by the Witchberry hills; on the other side, and behind, by the eminences in the park, which are high and steep, and all overspread with a lofty hanging wood. The lawn pressing to the foot, or creeping up the slopes of

these hills, and sometimes winding along into the depth of the wood, traces a beautiful outline to a sylvan scene, already rich to luxuriance in massiness of foliage, and stateliness of growth.

"But though the wood appears to be entire, it in reality opens frequently into lawns, which occupy much of the space within it: in the number, the variety, and the beauty of these lawns, in the shades of the separations between them, in their beauties also, and their varieties, the glory of Hagley consists . . . The boundary of one is described by a few careless lines; that of another is composed of many parts, very different and very irregular; and the ground is never flat, but falls sometimes in steep descents, sometimes in gentle declivities, waves along easy swells, or is thrown into broken inequalities, with endless variety.

"An octagon seat, sacred to the memory of Thomson, erected on his favourite spot, stands on the brow of a steep; a mead winds along the valley beneath, till it is lost on either hand between some trees; opposite to the seat, a noble wood crowns the top, and feathers down to the bottom, of a large, oval, swelling hill; as it descends on one side, the distant country becomes the offskip; over the fall on the other side the Clent hills appear; a dusky antique tower stands just below them, at the extremity of the wood; and in the midst of it is seen a Doric portico, called Pope's Building, with part of the lawn before it; the scene is very simple; the principle features are great; they prevail over all the rest, and are intimately connected with each other . . .

"At the end of the valley . . . in an obscure corner, and shut out from all view, is a hermitage, composed of roots and of moss; high banks, and a thick covert darkened with horse-chesnuts, confine the sequestered spot; a little rill trickles through it, and two small pieces of water occupy the bottom; they are seen on one side through groupes of trees; the other is open, but covered with fern; this valley is the extremity of the park, and the Clent hills rise in all their irregularities immediately above it . . ."

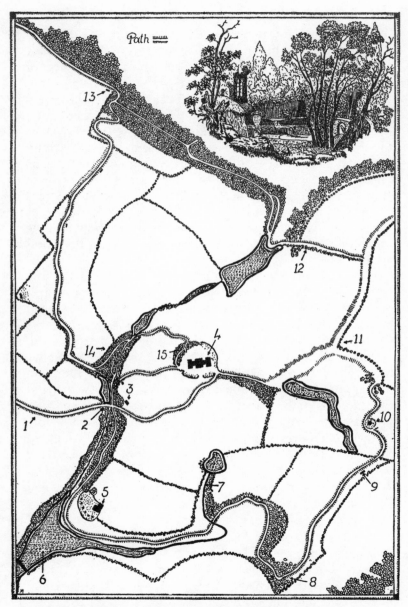

The plan of a landscape garden of the middle of the eighteenth century

THE LEASOWES

An Eighteenth-century Landscape Garden

Key

There are no walls to hide this garden from the lane (1) which leads to the estate. One can go down towards a small pool (2), of which there are five linked by a stream. Beyond it is a curious little building (3) made from the roots of big old trees. From here one sees the house (4), divided from the fields by a ha-ha. Near the wood are ruins of a mediaeval priory (5) and a large sheet of water (6), almost a lake. Next, the path crosses a stream below the "fairy vision" of a cascade (7). A seat (8) is placed to give a view of the priory, and another seat (9) looks upon a distant object like an Egyptian pyramid, which is the smelting house of a glass works. On a giant goblet (10) is inscribed the old Shropshire toast: "To all friends around the Wrekin." A wicket gate (11) leads to wilder ground. Nearby is a lovers' walk (12) and another pool. (13) is again a seat. Virgil's Grove (14) is a wood of deep gloom and quiet. (15) is a shrubbery.

We should remember the gardens of Le Nôtre, or that designed by Wise at Melbourne, and compare them with Hagley. What a revolution has been brought about by William Kent! And we have seen that the odd thing is that he was not a gardener. Apart from his early years, he was an architect and a designer. Yet those early years when he was a painter probably account for much of his success. For then it was that he learned the secrets of the Italian art of composing pictures of landscapes in the idealised manner, practised by the idols of the day, Salvator Rosa and Claude.

There is little more to be told of Kent's life. The Yorkshire lad became so haughty in his bearing that he was nicknamed "The Signor". He grew very stout in his prosperity, and so far lost his Yorkshire pride that he boasted about his Italian constitution being unsuited to the English climate.

In 1748, we read, "high feeding and an inactive life" brought on an illness from which he did not recover.

The most important result of Kent's work was, of course, that flowering plants became of less importance; the gayness of the fashionable gardens was banished from around the house into the distant kitchen garden. Buildings and obelisks now caught the eye, not colour. The trees that were so extensively planted were the native English kinds—the flowering trees and most of the conifers that we now grow were, of course, unknown in his time.

The old gardens of the great disappeared and were turned into landscape—they became "a green thought in a green shade" instead of an embroidery in hedges and flowers.

LANCELOT BROWN

While Kent was working at Stowe, a young man named Lancelot Brown was appointed head gardener. He had entered the gardens in 1740, full of ambition, but had been put to work in the kitchen garden—which, as we have seen, was now the most inferior part of the place. However, he was both very capable and, coming from the north country, had a way with him and did not suffer from undue modesty. Before long, therefore, he was the practical man, the head gardener, who was in charge of making the alterations that Kent planned.

His parents were very humble people from Kirkharle, in Northumberland. Little is known about them. The boy had the advantage of a good education, for the neighbouring school was excellent. At the age of sixteen he was taken on in the gardens of one of the neighbouring gentry. Here he worked for some years, becoming well grounded in the practice of gardening—and so gaining an advantage that Kent and his fellow-enthusiasts were without.

Feeling at last that he was well qualified, Brown decided to come south and seek his fortune. Breaking away from his happy family circle, he went to Wotton, a small estate near Woodstock in Oxfordshire. The owner of this was Sir Richard Grenville—brother-in-law to Lord Cobham of Stowe. And we can assume that it was through this connection that the ambitious young gardener gained employment in the gardens about which so many people were talking.

There is no doubt that Brown, far excelling Kent in practical ability and in the mechanics of garden *making*, learned from him at Stowe the principles of garden *design*. Before long we find that he was being allowed to use this knowledge to "improve" the old-fashioned gardens of some of the friends of his employer. One of the first works that he undertook was to modernise the gardens of Lord Brooke at Warwick Castle—with results that we can see today, in a fine situation for a picturesque garden.

In 1744 Brown married, and in due course the first of his family was born—a boy named after his father Lancelot. His marriage was successful and his family life happy.

At this stage of his career we begin to find published references to his work: gardens "well laid out by one Brown, who has set up on a few ideas of Kent" is typical of the kind of comment that we read. His ability and powers of organisation clearly made it possible for him to run the still increasing gardens at Stowe with admirable efficiency as well as undertaking more outside work. So that soon after Lord Cobham died, in 1749, Brown moved again, this time to Hammersmith, and set up as a full-time garden designer. Full-time, indeed, describes his situation, for from now on, until the day of his death, he moved from one client to another, improving old or laying out new gardens in rapid succession.

The immediate impression that his portrait gives is of liveliness and friendliness—a smallish man with a long nose, and dark eyes that are breaking into a smile under bushy eyebrows—the merry face of a man who had interesting and amusing talk. There was nothing of Kent's "Italian constitution" about Brown—no airs and graces. If you wanted a lake made, it wouldn't be long before his quick mind found the way to do it. Not a great designer or painter of landscapes himself, perhaps, but very good at turning existing landscapes into something nearer perfection or bringing them to greater magnificence—an "improver" of nature.

"Yes," he would say, standing with some great nobleman who had called him in, "the place has capabilities of improvement, great capabilities." So he gained the name by which he is always known, "Capability" Brown. It was a popular nickname—for when his son went to school (not to a Northumberland grammar school, but Eton College—along with the sons of his father's friends) he too was called "Capey".

"Capability" travelled the countryside visiting his patrons, regardless of the weather or the state of his own health (he was often wheezing from asthma). He would ride round the estate that he was to turn into a "picture" and quickly devise how this was to be done: a bare hillside planted with clumps of trees; half a wood here cut down to disclose a distant vista that had remained unsuspected until seen by his quick eye; a useless, swampy field there turned into a lake by a dam thrown across a trickling stream. His plans quickly made and approved, he would then give precise directions for their accomplishment—for he was first of all a practical and experienced gardener.

At some places he was concerned with buildings that were required in his schemes, either as features or eye-catchers, and at others with considerable additions to the houses of his patrons. He even designed a number of houses himself—successful good sound places but not very distinguished. Close neighbours of his were the Hollands, a family that had been builders for generations. They knew the practical side of building as Brown knew all about gardening. Browns and Hollands became intimate friends—and Lancelot Brown and Mr. Holland found each other very helpful in their respective businesses. Eventually Brown took on Mr. Holland's son, Henry, as an assistant. He proved of great help to his master—a debt duly repaid when "Capability" launched him among his own wide circle of patrons as an architect on his own account—and also by becoming his father-in-law.

Having taken a closer look at the successful Northumbrian, repeatedly leaving his happy family circle and his friends to travel away to one of his seemingly endless engagements to "improve", we should look at his achievements as a garden designer and find out why we regard him as a pioneer. Today it is in many ways much less easy for us to grasp his importance than it was for those living in his time. Carrying on from where Kent left off, he did, it is true, obliterate most of the great formal gardens of England, cut down avenues (not so many as his enemies made out), and banish flowers and fruit to within concealed walled gardens. But that was what he did away with; it is the originality of his often vast schemes of planning and planting that we now find difficult to grasp. The reason is surprising, for much that we regard as the typical English scene—the park, gently sloping down to its placid lake, clumps of fine old trees, and surrounding hills with woodlands curving around them (broken here to disclose a distant church, there to show a ruined castle)—is, in fact, not "nature" at all, but the product of the fertile mind of "Capability" and much heavy work by gangs of labourers. Countless acres around the country homes of the British nobility and gentry of the eighteenth century were so planned by him, and many more by those working in his manner. Of course, this sameness of his work is a failing: he had not the genius of Kent or of some amateur designers of the day who devoted years of work to perfecting their own bits of landscapes. Brown worked like a mass-producer, but Britain is more beautiful as a result.

We can gain some measure of his skill and ability by examining two of his best-known undertakings. Blenheim Palace was, as is well known, built to the plans of Sir John Vanbrugh and Nicholas Hawksmore for the Duke of Marlborough—one of the most magnificent buildings in England. The great enterprise had ended in disagreements and shortage of money. The approach to the palace crossed a small river valley, and here Vanbrugh embarked on one of his most extravagant features—a broad triumphal bridge. Beneath it were to be splendidly furnished rooms.

This massive and handsome structure was hardly the appropriate means of crossing a brook-like river trickling through an insignificant valley—but it was all that Vanbrugh could find across which to throw a bridge on a scale commensurate with the Duke's triumphs and fortune. Little had been done to make the park surrounding the new palace an appropriate setting for one of the masterpieces of English architecture. The calculated grandeur of the palace was unmatched by its undistinguished surroundings.

When the Duke and all those principally concerned in the building of Blenheim had been dead some years, "Capability" was called in to bring his improving talents to bear on the park. In this case he took his opportunity and handled the work magnificently. His experienced eye saw just where the trivial river might be dammed and the little valley turned into a fine winding lake (that might even be mistaken for a broad river). The waters as they rose and spread submerged the pillars of the bridge until one upper part alone remained above the flood. The bridge (or so it seemed) was now flung triumphantly over a mighty stream. ("The River Thames will never forgive me for this,"

Brown said.) The raggle-taggle woods in the park soon disappeared and were replaced by those groups and bands of trees that we now see—all so cunningly planted as to seem "nature" itself.

One other of Brown's triumphs in making the "ideal aspects of nature triumph over herself as she so often really is" may be seen at Croome Court. This was the home of the Earls of Coventry. The house was old, set in a flat and damp corner of Worcestershire, where the junction of the Rivers Avon and Severn form an angle. George William, the sixth earl, decided to turn his swampy park into a modern garden. Brown was called in. With great skill he drained the land by drawing off the surplus water into a new lake by cutting an artificial river. Then he was able to lay out the grounds in his usual manner—with walks, trees and a variety of temples, bridges and other "eye-catchers". As was written shortly after this had been accomplished: "It has been well observed of this now charming place, that nature has contributed but little to its beauties; but that the powers of art, and the transcendent skill of Brown, have been blessed with uncommon success." An inscription in the garden reads:

To the memory of Lancelot Brown
Who by the power of his inimitable genius formed
this garden scene out of a morass.

Nor should we forget his patron, who is said to have spent £400,000 on acquiring his fame as the draining, planting and building earl!

In spite of his success and almost universal employment by the great personages of the day, "Capability" met with some opposition. First there were those who kept their affection for the old type of formal garden; fortunately, a few of these (generally in out-of-the-way places) resisted the change in fashion. It is through them that we are still able to find an occasional formal garden remaining. More important, but not very effective, was that coming from the eminent and successful architect Sir William Chambers. He comes on to our stage again in the story of Kew Gardens, but since he made a personal attack on Brown, we must introduce him here.

In his youth Chambers went to China; so, when he wished to launch an attack on Brown, he disguised it in a booklet called *A Dissertation on Oriental Gardening*. This is a remarkable essay, foreshadowing the kind of planting, with carefully blended colour schemes, that did not come into fashion until late-Victorian days. But, in spite of its title, the book in reality was no more Chinese in outlook than Chambers was a Chinaman; it was a thinly veiled attack on "Capability" and his system. "Chinese gardeners are not only botanists, but also painters and philosophers, having a thorough knowledge of the human mind and the arts . . ."—a pretty good dig at the plain Northumbrian. Or of the visitor to one of Brown's gardens, finding

> "a large green field, scattered over with a few straggling trees . . . he finds a little serpentine path, twining in regular S's along which he wanders, roasted by the sun, so that he resolves to see no more, but vain resolution! there is but one path; he must either drag on to the end, or return back by the tedious way he came."

Chambers certainly spotted all the weaknesses both in Brown's personality and his designs. Today his description of the typical Brown garden seems very exaggerated, particularly when we learn that on one estate Brown planted over a hundred thousand oaks and pines. Yet he did fell and clear a lot of timber; we are inclined to forget that at the time of Chambers these fellings would be very obvious and the thousands of young trees he planted no more than slender saplings. As the plantations were of slow-growing English trees, particularly oaks, Brown and his patrons never saw their "landscapes" in their full maturity as we know them—they lived only in the mind's eye. The work of the designer and the support of his patrons was a creative act of faith, to be enjoyed in full by many succeeding generations.

The attacks that Brown suffered did not check his successful career. As to Chambers, since he devoted his own prosperous life entirely to architecture, we cannot know how his theories of gardening would have worked out in practice: possibly a sad loss.

In 1764 Brown reached the summit of his professional career on his appointment as a Royal Gardener. He now moved from Hammersmith to Wilderness House, near Hampton Court—for it was there that he was given charge of the gardens—and made new friends among those who lived in the district, including the actor David Garrick and his circle.

Three years later he bought a country estate in Huntingdonshire, becoming the lord of the manor. And this gives us an opportunity to show that Brown was not such a bigoted enthusiast for his own ideas as some would make out. For his manor house, at Fenstanton, was a charming little place in the old-fashioned manner, with clipped yew hedges surrounding the formal garden. Brown, the alleged enemy of all these things, left the old place unchanged and unimproved. Shortly after, he became High Sheriff of Huntingdonshire; the gardener's boy from Kirkharle was now truly one of the landed gentry.

His visits to Fenstanton had one very happy result. The place is not far from Cambridge, and Brown soon found himself among a new and different circle of friends and acquaintances—the dons of the University. For them he undertook the landscaping and planting of the "Backs"—that part of the University by the river. The most lovely place that we now enjoy is surely one of his best memorials—though it led to some embarrassment at the time. Brown did not ask for the large fee which he would normally have received, and the authorities were diffident about offering money to a High Sheriff. The problem was solved when the University presented him with a handsome piece of silver plate.

Brown, as he passed into old age, must have been a happy as well as a successful man. He saw his son-in-law, Henry Holland, who had first worked with him as assistant, launched on his own successful career as the architect of many famous and delightful buildings. His eldest son, Lancelot, took to politics and became Member of Parliament for Huntingdonshire. Another son, John, was doing well in the Navy, rising to the rank of admiral. Yet probably nothing gave him more pleasure than the friendship of some of his patrons. This sometimes went far beyond that usually enjoyed between employer and employed. Brown's sagacity was equalled by his integrity. Often he might have received far larger sums than he did for his services. But invariably he worked to a fixed scale of fees; when carrying out the constructional work himself, he saw to it that his clients got good value for their money. On several occasions he is known to have returned fees in excess of what he considered were his due.

Brown's patrons included, from the King downwards, the most important political figures of the day, often bitterly opposed to one another. There is no doubt that Brown, trusted by both sides, was sometimes a go-between among these opposing factions.

The Earl of Chatham and his family were among his close friends. When the Earl had been William Pitt, Brown had worked for him at his home, Burton Pynsent, in Somerset. The great statesman suffered long spells of illness and melancholy, and periods of bitter frustration as a politician. His gardens, on which he spent extravagantly, no doubt gave him relief and relaxation. As he grew older and iller, a martyr to gout, a difficult and at times terrifying figure, his friendship with Brown remained unruffled, and he was certainly one of those for whom Brown acted as intermediary.

There is a story of the two men meeting. As they parted, "Go you and adorn the country," said the Earl. "Go you and preserve it," Brown replied.

One morning at the beginning of February 1783, he went to call about some matter of business at the London house of his old friend and patron Lord Coventry. After returning to his home at Hampton Court, without warning he fell; in a few moments he was dead.

An entry made at the time in the diary of Horace Walpole, most critical and carping of men, sums up his work and character with insight. His genius, he said, was such and so great that it will be least remembered by men, for they will take it as the work of nature; but his truth, his integrity and his good humour will always hold a place in the memory of his friends.

HUMPHRY REPTON

William Kent began life with the intention of becoming a painter and ended it by making real landscapes. Lancelot Brown was gardener from first to last. The third of the trio who transformed much of the face of England seems to have had no particular ambitions as a young man and in middle age to have become a garden designer almost by chance. Humphry Repton was born at Bury St. Edmunds on 2nd May, 1752. His father, John, was a collector of taxes, which in those days was a profitable position. His mother came of a good old Suffolk family.

Humphry was the second son. In due course, he went to Bury Grammar School—a rough place of which in later life he had not happy recollections. Later his parents moved to Norwich and he went to the grammar school there.

John Repton was, of course, in a good position to know which trades and professions were prospering. It seems that he had no doubt that if his son wished to make a fortune, he should become a merchant dealing in Norwich manufactures with the Continent, particularly Holland.

So in 1764 Humphry went to that country to finish his education in a Dutch school. He lived in the home of one Zachary Hope, a wealthy and cultivated man whose family moved in the highest circles. Humphry was an attractive and accomplished youth, and from the people that he now met he gained a polish to his social graces as well as a knowledge of Dutch and Continental life.

Young though he was, letters home to the parents that he loved flowed freely from his pen. Even at this early age the sights and scenery particularly attracted his attention. One letter shows his youthful interest in gardens. Travelling by canal, he wrote, one sees right into the Dutch gardens, for they are designed to be looked into from the water, and without regard to privacy. What is surprising is that there are practically no flowers; the beds are arranged in patterns like embroidery edged with dwarf box hedges, and they are filled not with plants but coloured materials, such as red brick-dust, charcoal, yellow sand, chalk, coloured ores, green broken glass, and spars, all arranged to make a gay pattern.

The boy came home when he was sixteen. In later years he laughed at himself at this stage; he was, he assures us, no more than a dandy, his clothes considered above all, his heart in dancing and other social frivolities. Added to his vivacious manner were a sweet voice and skill as a flautist; he had some talent at sketching, too. In fact, he was a social success. In spite of this he had a determined nature; he fell in love with a certain Miss Clarke, but their parents forbade marriage as both were so young. Humphry never had any doubts about the matter, then or during the next forty and more years; the couple were married within a day or two of his coming of age, and lived happily ever after.

As had been planned by his father, he was in due course set up as

The work of Humphry Repton: a landscape garden (*above*) before and (*below*) after "improvement"

a merchant. At first the business was fairly successful. But from what we know of his later life, we suspect that neither his heart nor his interests were much concerned in dealing and shipping. Eventually, his undertaking became unprofitable—possibly because he lost the advice of his father, who had died. Being now reasonably well off, he withdrew from trade and lived the quiet life and discharged the duties of a country gentleman. His home was at Sustead, near Aylsham in Norfolk. Encouraged by his friend and schoolfellow, the famous botanist James Edward Smith, he developed an interest in botany and set about improving his own garden. A neighbour was William Windham, of Felbrigg, of ancient lineage in the county. He was a man of culture and intelligence and owner of a fine library. In it Repton studied botany and the arts to good effect. He was interested also in local history, visiting and making drawings of all the seats of the Norfolk gentry within reach of Sustead.

This happy and interesting country life was suddenly interrupted in a rather surprising way. In 1783 Windham accepted a high government post in Dublin, and invited Repton to travel with him to Ireland as his confidential secretary, and so to engage in another new career. An even greater surprise followed. After a month, Windham suddenly resigned his post and returned home, leaving his confidential secretary to carry on. For nearly two months until Windham's successor arrived, Repton therefore found himself occupying a position of consequence in the highest political and social circles of Dublin. Though not the kind of life he would have chosen, his many social talents made him a popular figure and he seems hugely to have enjoyed his short period of unsought and unexpected importance.

This short-lived venture over, he settled down at Hare Street, near Romford in Essex. Here he again set about improving his garden and bringing its layout and planting into line with his views, which, following much thought and study, were by now decisively formed.

He also embarked on a new business venture. A certain John Palmer had worked out a plan for improving the postal system by the introduction and use of special high-speed mail coaches. Repton joined with him in financing a business to put it into effect. The idea was somewhat in advance of its time and failed. Repton lost a substantial sum of money.

Now father of a large family, for the first time in his life he found himself in serious difficulties. No longer had he adequate independent means, he was middle-aged and had not been brought up in a profession to which he might turn for a living. An anxious time followed. One night, lying awake worrying about the future, he came to a conclusion. He was an amateur artist of talent, had spent much time studying houses and gardens. Further, he had acquired a good practical knowledge of botany and gardening. Lancelot Brown was dead. It was now clear to him what his future career should be—that of successor to "Capability" as landscape-gardener. He went soundly to sleep. Next morning, without further delay, he began writing to every one of his numerous acquaintances all over the kingdom announcing this intention.

Commissions came in almost at once. Within a year or two, he was well launched on a career comparable with Kent and Brown, whom he now joined to form the trio of masters of the English landscape school of gardening. This is surprising when we remember that he did not embark upon it until he was thirty-six years old. Before long he was working for patrons of great consequence, such as the Duke of Portland at Welbeck, in Nottinghamshire. Cobham Hall in Kent (which we find in *Pickwick Papers*) and Ashridge in Hertfordshire are other estates that he improved; Repton worked, too, for that enthusiastic planner and builder the Prince of Wales, later Prince Regent and finally George IV. For a time he was in partnership with John Nash, architect. Repton, when consulted, often included advice on the "improvement" of, or for additions to, the mansion on the estate; he also suggested additional buildings, bridges and so on. Nash, at that time a provincial architect of no great reputation, carried out this architectural work. By this means he gained the connection and patronage which soon brought him fame as the typical architect of the Regency period. Here we may remark how closely the work of the great landscape-gardeners was allied to architecture: Kent was himself an architect first and foremost; Lancelot Brown designed some houses himself, but was closely linked with his son-in-law, the architect Henry Holland, while Repton, as we have seen, was for a time partnered by Nash.

At the point where "Capability" left off, there Repton began—both in the sense of time and the manner in which he worked. The second

Lancelot Brown, now a Member of Parliament, went so far as to lend him his father's plans.

Repton was, however, a much more widely educated man than Brown or than Kent. He had studied both the arts and the sciences, and applied them to his gardening. We are in no doubt about his theories, for he wrote about them freely. *Observations on the Theory and Practice of Landscape Gardening* was the most handsome book that came from his pen, carrying some fine coloured plates and numerous diagrams.

He was a thorough man and worked on quite a different system from his predecessors. When called upon to "improve" an estate, he made a very complete examination of it, including a number of sketches. From this illustrated survey was prepared what he called a *Red Book*, which described the place as it was at present, pointing out the features good and bad—the good to be retained and emphasised, the bad to be removed or improved. To make his points clear, the *Red Book* included drawings of the principal views of the place as they were. Gummed to their edges were cut-out figures of the "improvements". These could be folded down over the first drawing: his client could then see the effect "before and after."

Though Repton carried on from the point where Brown left off, he later developed a style of his own. He brought back flower-gardens to the immediate surrounds of the mansion. In one of Brown's designs you stepped straight from the house into the "landscape"; Repton led you first into a flower-garden, which then merged gradually with the "landscape". We may recall his friendship with Sir J. E. Smith and his interest in botany, which inevitably meant that he moved among a circle of acquaintances who were keenly interested in individual plants as such. Neither Brown nor Kent had such an interest—the "picture" was all that they cared for. Another feature for which Repton was to some extent responsible was the introduction of ornamental cottages for housing the gardeners and estate workers; these he used to replace the useless "eye-catchers" of his predecessors.

Repton's success naturally made him a target for criticism. He himself described with amusement his surprise at reading attacks made upon his alleged design of gardens in which he had never set foot. A more serious enemy was, however, a learned, cultivated and very wealthy Herefordshire squire, Richard Payne Knight. While his shafts were directed at Repton personally, we can see now that it was more concerned with the typical "Capability" Brown landscape with its shaven lawns.

Knight wrote a long poem praising the virtues of the romantic, picturesque and colourful garden. Instead of the groomed park reaching to the walls of the house, he called for:

> The bright acacia, and the vivid plane,
> The rich laburnum with its golden chain;
> And all the variegated flow'ring race,
> That deck the garden, and the shrubb'ry grace,
> Should near to buildings, or to water grow,
> When bright reflections beam with equal glow,
> And blending vivid tints with vivid light,
> The whole in brilliant harmony unite . . .

Brown and Repton only gave him

> Prim gravel walks, through which we winding go,
> In endless serpentines that nothing show . . .

This was a little hard on Repton—or perhaps he took Knight's attack to heart, for certainly he did bring back colour, variety and novelty to the garden. He was at times almost a pioneer of the return to the Gothic and mediaeval styles that began to replace Classic architecture, so long the rule. He certainly toyed with designs in an Indian manner and his enthusiasm for verandahs, then a novelty from that country, helped to bring about their popularity.

Repton's life and work were an unqualified success, without a day's illness, until one January night in 1811. Escorting his daughters home from a dance, the carriage struck a snow-drift and overturned. He was seriously injured, and for a long time had to keep to his bed. Eventually he was able to work again, but with the knowledge that he was suffering from a condition that might cause his sudden death. He refused to let this deter him, and carried on cheerfully. At last, in March 1818, what the doctors had threatened took place: the last of the great landscape-gardeners fell and died as easily as he had passed through life.

> "To improve the scenery of a country, and to display its native beauties to advantage, is an art which originated in England, and has therefore been called *English Gardening*; . . . Gardening, in its more confined sense of horticulture, has likewise been brought to the greatest perfection in this country . . ."

So Repton justly claimed. Unlike Kent and Brown, eventually he strove to combine landscape and horticulture and so to be the first true Landscape-Gardener.

The effect that these three men had on the style of gardening throughout the world was singular; the English or landscape garden became as famous as the French formal garden. And to them, the first great country-planners, we owe much of our lovely British countryside.

CHAPTER 6

Poineers at Kew

It is often forgotten that the gardens at Kew are truly Royal Botanic Gardens—an official institution for the study of botany. The vast collection of trees, shrubs and plants, one of the largest in the world, has been got together for scientific purposes, yet thanks to those who, during the centuries, have brought the gardens into being, science has been combined with art; indeed, most of us visit the place for the reason its beauty appeals to us and not because it is a botanical establishment.

The gardens consist of two old estates, Richmond Lodge and Kew House, lying together on one side of the Thames. We need not bother with their long and interesting early history, except to note that, like Syon House across the river, both had included keen gardeners among their owners, and no doubt the existing fame of the garden was one of the reasons why Frederick, Prince of Wales, son of George II, and his wife, Princess Augusta, went to live at Kew House in 1730.

The Prince engaged William Kent to lay out the park. The Princess was keenly interested in botany and began to collect rare plants for the garden. Frederick, who died before his father, does not take up much space in our history books; they generally do no more than quote his father's comment on him: "the greatest ass, the greatest liar, and the greatest beast in all the world." Still, there is no doubt that he and Augusta made a fine garden in a fine park. But it would probably never have achieved its present fame but for a coincidence. One day in 1747 Frederick was at Egham races. Heavy rain stopped all sport. The Prince wanted a game of cards. The party was, however, one short. Someone went out and asked John, Earl of Bute, to make up. The Prince, who had never yet met him, was at once attracted by the Earl, who became his intimate friend and adviser.

The history books haven't got much good to say about the Earl either. You will read that he was later one of our most unsuccessful Prime Ministers. He became so unpopular among the people that in public he was always accompanied by a private bodyguard of toughs and prize-fighters. But he was an ardent botanist and gardener, a great collector of plants as well as a discerning patron of the arts and sciences. He had spent the first nine years of his married life studying the natural history on his own island of Bute. In 1751 the Prince of Wales died—it is said from an illness caused by a chill caught when walking in the garden—and Bute became confidential adviser to his widow. Since the Princess had moved into Kew House, she had, largely with his advice, made a very considerable collection of interesting plants. Now, as Dowager Princess, she devoted even more of her energies to the garden. With the Earl of Bute acting as a sort of director, Kew began its long career of fame as a centre of scientific gardening and the practical study of plants.

One of the most important traditions of Kew has been that science has always been happily united with art. The Princess, under the Earl's guidance, was responsible for the founding of this tradition. In 1759 a twenty-eight-year-old Scot from Lanarkshire, William Aiton, was appointed to manage the gardens. On coming to London a few years previously, he had been engaged by Philip Miller and was one of the young men trained by that famous gardener.

Aiton spent the rest of his life at Kew, tending and studying the rapidly increasing collections. Apart from being the first head gardener at Kew, his claim to fame lies in his production of the first of the catalogues of plants for which Kew has since become notable. With the help of other prominent botanists, Aiton spent sixteen years compiling a three-volumed *Hortus Kewensis*. Published in 1789, it was a list of the five thousand six hundred species of plants growing at Kew, just about four thousand more than Bobart grew at Oxford. It is particularly important to historians, for he gave great care to seeking out the dates at which the plants described were introduced into this country. Aiton died in 1793. He was a man "highly estimable for mildness, benevolence, piety and every domestic and social virtue", and founded the Kew tradition of practical skill in gardening combined with the knowledge and thoroughness of a good botanist. He was succeeded by his son, William Townsend Aiton.

Some of the trees that old Aiton planted can probably still be seen today, but there is no difficulty in identifying the work of the architect who was called in by the Princess on Bute's recommendation to diversify the gardens; indeed, it is impossible to miss seeing Sir William Chambers' gay and fantastic pagoda that tapers layer upon layer high up among the tree-tops.

Chambers, whom we have met before as the enemy of "Capability" Brown, after an adventurous youth during which he had visited China and the East in Swedish ships, settled down to become an architect. Some of his earliest work was done at Kew. In addition to the pagoda, he designed an imitation Roman arch and several delightful little summer houses or arbours in the style of classical temples. Today his Temple of the Sun, standing on its daffodil- and shrub-planted mound, is still one of Kew's most charming sights. He designed, too, the "Great Stove", which for a long time remained the biggest hot-house in England. Sir William, as we have read, was one of the critics of the "landscape" style of gardening with its lack of flowers which was then all the fashion. To him a garden meant a place full of the carefully blended colours of flowers, of delightful buildings, all brought together in an ingenious and entertaining plan—a place to fascinate botanists, painters and philosophers, a garden combining all the arts. These ideas about garden design were in advance of his time, and thus almost bring him into the ranks of pioneers. His work was particularly suitable to Kew, as we can see today—though it was not approved by the highbrows of the day. "There is little taste or invention shown," wrote Horace Walpole of the gardens.

When the Dowager Princess Augusta died, George III (who had always been interested in his sister-in-law's garden) bought the adjoining estate of Richmond House and added it to the Kew estate, so making another important contribution to the gardens as we know them today. The Earl of Bute became more and more involved in politics—eventually to die, it is said, from the results of a fall when trying to reach a rare plant. Sir Joseph Banks now replaced him as the virtual director of the gardens, one of the most important among his many other activities. Under his guidance, Kew spread its activities still further afield—Francis Masson went to the Cape of Good Hope to collect plants for the garden, and a Kew man, David Nelson, was the botanist and gardener who went as expert on Captain Bligh's disastrous expedition in the *Bounty*. His aim was to introduce the breadfruit tree to the West Indies.

In the first years of the nineteenth century the reputation of Kew rose still higher, its fame spread wider. Then, within a few years, all changed. The old King went mad and the Prince Regent was not interested in gardens. Sir Joseph Banks became aged and inactive. The popular fashion for botany waned, to be replaced by other newer and more exciting developments of science. Wars raged. Kew Gardens, now shorn of their former glory, were only kept going by the loyalty of a few devoted servants, foremost of whom was William Townsend Aiton, the King's gardener.

Several influential people made noble efforts to right the situation, but no action was taken. The gardens were, of course, still the property of the sovereign and court officials preferred to use them for other than scientific purposes. A committee was formed to urge the need of an Empire Botanic Garden, with an independent, paid director (Bute and Banks had given their services voluntarily). But nothing was done.

At the beginning of Queen Victoria's reign the time came when old Aiton's son was himself aged and was due for retirement. What was to happen to the gardens now? Who would take on the thankless task of keeping the botanical collection going when the wish of those in authority was to turn the whole place into a pleasure garden?

Oddly enough, the professor of botany at Glasgow University, W. J. Hooker, began to make inquiries about obtaining the unenviable position soon to be vacant. He was, in fact, anxious to get back from the north to be near London again and thought Aiton's job might suit him.

Almost more important, the then Duke of Bedford (like others of his line, a fine patron of the natural sciences) was now determined to use his powers behind the scenes to further the formation of a national botanical garden at Kew. The Duke and his friends also thought that Hooker was just the man to be the first director.

We need not go into the stupid and obstinate opposition which the Duke was the prime mover in overcoming. He had, unhappily, died before he could see the triumph of his efforts on the appointment of Hooker in 1842. No chance or accident brought about this, the most important event in the history of the gardens; persistence and planning won the day.

William Jackson Hooker is one of the greatest figures in the history of scientific gardening. It is to him above all others that we owe Kew Gardens in their present form. He could well claim a place among pioneer botanists, or as a pioneer in the enlightened management of scientific institutions—but it is because he finally combined and brought all these abilities to the service of gardening and the cultivation of plants that he has a place of particular importance in this book.

The Hookers were a Devonshire family, but "W. J.'s" father had moved to Norwich. He must have been interested in plants, for he owned a fine collection of succulents—the cultivation of which, we read, was then a "favourite pursuit of his fellow-citizens".

Young Hooker was brought up in comfortable circumstances, and his only trouble seems to have been that he had such an extreme dislike of taking life that even the sight of blood made him feel ill. But as we shall see, this did not stop him undertaking arduous and dangerous expeditions. From childhood he was an enthusiastic student of insects and birds, but perhaps it was his dislike of killing specimens that eventually made him take most keenly to botany. As a young man he went to study estate management with a gentleman farmer, but having the means to be independent, soon became principally engaged as an amateur naturalist. Soon after he was twenty-one, so considerable was his reputation that one of the most learned societies in London elected him to its fellowship. In addition, he was a talented artist.

His interests soon brought him into touch with two men who later influenced his career considerably. The first was Dawson Turner, of Yarmouth, a rich banker who devoted much of his time to studying natural history. Hooker helped him in his study of mosses. Then, on his visits to London, his ability was soon recognised by Sir Joseph Banks, who was eventually to introduce him to a professional career.

In the meantime Hooker travelled widely. He was one of the first to study the living native plants of the remote parts of Scotland. They were then practically unvisited by Englishmen—let alone botanists. The difficulties of travel and often the hostility of the natives were comparable with those met today in the more outlandish parts of the modern world. At one time Hooker was taken up as a foreign spy.

In 1809, through the influence of Banks, he was able to make a botanising trip to Iceland. This turned out to be an odd and exciting adventure. At that time Iceland belonged to Denmark, and Denmark was at war with England. But there was valuable trade to be done between Iceland and England, and the expedition on which Hooker sailed was a private venture for the purpose of bringing this about. One of the party was a Mr. Jorgensen—a Dane who knew a good deal about Iceland and its trade. He had spent much of his youth in England, and greatly admired the English—but as a Dane he had fought loyally for his ally France until captured by the British during a naval battle.

The travellers arrived safely in Iceland, and Hooker carefully studied the hot springs, the customs of the people, and in particular plants (discovering a number not previously known to exist). Meanwhile, the surprising Mr. Jorgensen brought about a bloodless revolution, remodelled the laws for the benefit of the natives, improved the education of the people, and set the government of the island on a new footing. All this having been accomplished quite speedily, the party returned in two ships laden with Icelandic produce. That carrying Hooker and his collections sailed first. They were ordered not to take the direct route, but to go rather a long way round to avoid certain dangerous rocks. In the book that Hooker afterwards wrote describing his journey, he relates how, with a fair wind and fine weather, they sailed expecting a good quick voyage home. Jorgensen's party, in *Orion*, was to follow a day or two later.

At six o'clock one morning, when twenty leagues off the rocky and inhospitable coast, from which a fresh breeze was blowing, the cargo of tallow on Hooker's boat was found to be on fire. There was no hope whatever of reaching land, and in that unfrequented sea, none of rescue.

Hooker's own simple words are eloquent: "No one who has not been in a similar situation can have an idea what we felt." That is all.

Then the unbelievable happened. The sails of *Orion* appeared on the horizon, and soon all on board were saved. The extraordinary Mr. Jorgensen, among his other qualities being that of daring seaman, had taken charge of the ship as soon as she had left port and insisted on sailing the short cut through the dangerous rocks.

Thus the life of the future Director of Kew was saved, but he lost all his possessions and collections except a few pages of his diary and an Icelandic girl's wedding dress! Yet his memory was so remarkable that his record of the voyage is full of detail.

Hooker's next expedition was to have been a visit to Ceylon. To acquaint himself with the plants that he would be likely to find there, he made something like two thousand small copies from paintings of native plants made by Indians. This labour was, however, in vain: a revolution broke out in Ceylon and the voyage was called off. So during the next year or two he contented himself with botanical explorations in Devon, Cornwall and the Scilly Isles.

In 1815 he married the daughter of his old friend Dawson Turner. They spent a long honeymoon wandering through the Lake District and then sailed across to Ireland. His wife had many of his interests, and was also an accomplished amateur artist. We can imagine their happiness in collecting plants and studying wild life. And instead of taking hurried snap-shots as we do, they sat down and made sketches of the old buildings and scenery, so observing and enjoying their intimate details in a manner unknown to us.

The pair settled down at Halesworth in Suffolk, where Hooker owned a brewery. It seems that he was not a very good businessman. For one thing, his scientific work took up most of his time, Also, the results of his studies were printed with illustrations on a lavish scale at his own expense, at a heavy loss. So he decided to give up business and take on some sort of paid work more closely connected with his real interests. The professorship of botany at Glasgow University became vacant. An added attraction was a botanical garden under the control of the professor. Once again Sir Joseph Banks acted the fairy godfather, and through his influence Hooker obtained the professorship.

At Glasgow he stayed for twenty years. The school of botany and the botanic garden soon grew to fame under his direction. His abilities as an organiser and administrator and a man of forceful and winning character now began to shine. In his portrait he is a tall, dark, slim, erect man with a clear and penetrating gaze. We are not surprised to learn that he could walk sixty miles in a day without tiring. At Glasgow, after the week-end at his country home, he walked the twenty-two miles to University every Monday morning to be in his place by eight o'clock. This, then, was the man who in 1842 was appointed to take charge of that small part of the Royal Kew and Richmond estates now set aside as our first national botanic garden.

Hooker set to work to bring back to the dimmed name of Kew the fame and lustre of half a century before.

He was able to carry forward from the victory that the Duke of Bedford and his friends had won without difficulty; for his was a personality that soon won over those obstinate politicians and officials still prepared to make difficulties. Moreover, he won the support of Queen Victoria and the Prince Consort—who were personally responsible for saving the fine trees in the park (then outside the gardens) from being felled.

Hooker at once opened the gardens to the public, so that people could see for themselves what was being done. In this first year there were 9,000 visitors; in the last year of his directorship 73,000.

Men from Kew again sailed on Admiralty and other expeditions to collect and study plants. Under the guiding direction of Hooker they went to New Grenada, California, Oregon, Japan, Formosa, Korea, the Cameroons, Gaboon River, Fernando Po, the Niger, Zambesi, East Africa, Madagascar, the Himalaya, Canada, British Columbia, Arctic America, Fiji Islands, Torres Straits, the Pacific Islands, Ecuador and the Azores. What an amazing catalogue of places—and probably I have missed some in making it! No wonder the reputation of Kew soared again, not only within the Empire, but throughout the world, as Hooker tirelessly worked behind the scenes to ensure that no important expedition of survey or exploration set out without a Kew botanist on the staff.

The work of these men resulted in the formation of a huge collection or "herbarium" of dried and pressed specimens, which were classified and from which invaluable "floras", or catalogues, of the plants growing throughout the Empire were later compiled. Kew became a gigantic clearing-house of information and an international centre of botanical study.

Hooker was responsible, too, for ensuring that as many of these plants as possible were grown in the gardens, so that the living thing as well as the botanist's specimen could be studied. He formed the first large collection of hardy herbaceous plants. At the other extreme he brought about the building of the Palm House, from the designs of Decimus Burton. For years it was the biggest greenhouse ever erected. The tropical aquarium built for the giant Amazonian water lily, which so thrilled the Victorians, was another of his undertakings.

It was due to his foresight and planning, too, that the seeds of the tree bearing "Peruvian bark", which yields quinine, the invaluable drug used for treating tropical fevers, were collected in the Andes mountains of South America. From them, trees were raised and planted in Ceylon and other parts of the Empire. When they had reached maturity, the price of quinine fell from *12s.* to *1s.* an ounce within a few years.

He called in the architect Nesfield to plan the clearings which opened the long sweeping vistas between the trees; he saw that a disused gravel pit could be turned into a lake, and planned the great collections of trees in the Pinetum and elsewhere. It was he who first encouraged the nesting of birds and made the gardens a sanctuary for wild life.

So when on an August day in 1865 Sir William Jackson Hooker died, having worked for Kew until a few days before, scientists and gardeners throughout the world mourned the passing of a great man and a pioneer of scientific horticulture.

CHAPTER 7

Pioneers of a Gardeners' Society

The Royal Horticultural Society—known to gardeners everywhere as the "R.H.S."—has today a membership of many thousands. At its halls in Westminster plants of all kinds—flowers, vegetables, fruit—are exhibited regularly throughout the year and the best selected and distinguished by awards. At Westminster, too, is housed the Lindley Library, the most famous gardeners' library in the world. At Wisley, in Surrey, the Society owns some 250 acres of land. Here are gardens of every type growing plants of practically every kind that will live in its climate. There are test-grounds where plants, both flowers and vegetables, are tried out so that the best may be selected and given awards that will indicate their merit to the gardeners of the world. We find, too, laboratories for scientific research and a hostel for the students who go there to study. The activities of the Society at Wisley and elsewhere are on an immense scale.

This organisation began at a meeting of seven at Hatchard's bookshop in Piccadilly on 7th March, 1804, "for the purpose of forming a Society for the Improvement of Horticulture." It might have been noticed then that these seven men came from almost as many callings and ranks in society, from the dilettante to the president of the Royal Society, from the aristocrat to the one-time garden boy. Gardening bridged all social gulfs and brought together those of different callings.

One of them was John Wedgwood, a son of the great Josiah, the potter who brought fame to the name of Wedgwood ware. John had been brought up in that circle of families centred in Staffordshire, all on terms of intimate friendship, and often intermarried, which surely did more than any other collection of human beings to bring about the modern world. He would know well, for instance, Boulton—that pioneering genius of the best aspects of industrialisation and mass production, the brilliant talent-spotter who picked James Watt and the invention of the steam-engine. And then that extraordinary and delightful character, the doctor, poet, botanist and amateur philosopher Erasmus Darwin, who sketched the scheme of evolution that was later to be worked out by his grandson, Charles Darwin.

John Wedgwood was sent to Edinburgh University, travelled extensively, and studied art under Flaxman—trained (as, alas, people are no longer trained) both in the arts and sciences, the graces learned by travel added, with a view to joining his father in the pottery. After a year or two, however, he left Staffordshire and came to live in London, where he shortly married a beautiful wife. When they set up house, he made the first of his interesting gardens. We know quite a lot about him as a gardener from his garden notebook made when he later lived at Kingscote in Gloucestershire, which still exists. He was a collector and successful cultivator of unusual plants, and made careful records of his experiments.

We can presume that at an early stage in his gardening he had, as we all do, gone to an older and experienced man for practical advice. His choice had fallen on William Forsyth, George III's gardener at Kensington and St. James's—a very prominent and, from his position, influential man in the horticultural world.

It was because of this, no doubt, that John Wedgwood chose William Forsyth as the man to whom he first disclosed the plan that he had formed. In 1801 he sent him a letter. "I have," he wrote, "been turning my attention to the formation of a Horticultural Society." Wedgwood came from a family of practical business men, and it is not surprising that draft rules were included in this letter—the letter that counts, therefore, as the first definite proposal for the beginning of the Society and which resulted three years later in the meeting which has been described. When the Society was formed he became its first treasurer.

Before long, however, he moved from London and spent the rest of his life rather restlessly changing from one house to another—but always making gardens. He was little more than a dilettante, but he was the founder of the Society.

From a cultured English gentleman we turn to Forsyth, a dogged, opinionated and undoubtedly capable little Scot, who had gone far since his obscure early days in Aberdeenshire. Little is known about him till he turned up in England working at the Apothecaries' Garden in Chelsea under Philip Miller. Later, he was gardener at Syon House, not far from Kew, where the Duke of Northumberland had gardens famed for their trees and shrubs (many of which can still be seen). Then, Miller retiring from Chelsea, the pushful Forsyth got his job. He at once started reorganising the venerable Chelsea garden. Famous old trees came down. He began to exchange plants with other gardeners and so added greatly to the collections. One of the first rock-gardens in history was built with old stones from the Tower of London and a quantity of lava brought from Iceland by Mr. Joseph Banks. Another example of these go-ahead methods—and this time one not far removed from fraud—was his invention of "Forsyth's Plaister". For a number of years our navy had been very active—the names of Rodney and Hood belong to this period, and the battle of Trafalgar was fought in the year after this meeting of the R.H.S. There was, as is usual in times of war, an outcry over the shortage of timber, particularly oak for shipbuilding. Much of the timber in our forests was old and decaying. Forsyth claimed to have invented a "plaister"—a slimy concoction that must have been revolting to handle—which, when applied in a certain way to derelict trees, would, he claimed, render them "as fit for the navy as though they never had been injured." Forsyth, of course, kept the formula of this almost magic paste to himself. But the possibilities of the invention were considered so great that the Houses of Parliament formed a joint Commission to investigate Forsyth's claims, and, if they were proved, to agree on a sum to be offered to him to disclose his secret "in order to diffuse the benefits of this discovery throughout the kingdom". If you have ever seen a portrait showing the keen, large-eyed, questing-nosed and lively-mouthed face of Forsyth, you will not be surprised to learn that he got his money, had his secret published in *The London Gazette*, and also did very well out of a book that he wrote about his own methods of using it. A number of prominent gardeners showed plainly that the invention was useless, including Thomas Knight, one of those present at the meeting. But Forsyth was not the type of man to fall out with anyone of Knight's standing, particularly as he was anxious to secure a high office in the Society about to be formed, which he would surely have used to his own benefit and those of his friends. His hopes, however, ended with his death within a few months of the meeting. There is no doubt that, whatever his failings, he was a fine gardener with high ambitions for the future of horticulture, earning his title as a pioneer—and worthy of a thought each spring as the flowers of *Forsythia*, named after him, open in thousands of gardens.

We turn now to a man who is clearly of a different type from the two that we have described—the baronet, Sir Joseph Banks. He was immensely wealthy, a power behind the scenes ("the autocrat of the philosophers"), courageous and adventurous, not only a pioneer himself but a patron and supporter of many another not so fortunately placed. At the time of the meeting he had already occupied the most honoured and consequential position in the scientific world—the presidency of the Royal Society—for over a quarter of a century.

Banks was the son of a wealthy man with large estates in Lincolnshire, but was born in London. He was at both Eton and Harrow, where, it seems, he behaved in the usual manner of youths with lots of money. Then one day (so the story goes) he was returning from a bathing party in the Thames, where he had lingered behind his companions, when he noticed for the first time the beauty and variety of the flowers in the hedgerows of the lanes. He thereupon decided to devote the rest of his life to their study.

Whether this story is true or not, by the time he entered Christ Church, Oxford, the pursuit of natural history had become the main object of his unbounded energy, and so it continued to be until the end of his long life. His father died just about the time that Banks came of age, and thenceforth he had ample means with which to follow his interests. Within a year or two he had made a trip to Newfoundland and Labrador, bringing back a rich collection of plants and insects.

In 1768 Lieut. James Cook, who had distinguished himself as a

Forsythia, named to commemorate William Forsyth, a founder of the
Royal Horticultural Society. The species on the left (*F. viridissima*)
introduced by Robert Fortune

navigator, surveyor and something of an astronomer, was appointed to conduct an expedition to carry out important astronomical and geographical investigations in the South Pacific Ocean—where Australia was then an almost unexplored land and New Zealand little more than a name. Banks saw that here was an opportunity to pursue his passion for natural history into an almost unknown and undiscovered world. Influence with friends at the Admiralty enabled him to join the expedition, taking an eminent and experienced scientist, Dr. Solander, as his assistant, and a staff of artists who were to become the first to depict the plants, animals and natural scenery of the new land. This journey, which lasted for three years, is of course well known in history as the voyage of the *Endeavour*. The voyage was full of hardship and adventure, as well as difficulties overcome by the tenacity of purpose and powers of leadership shown by Cook and Banks.

A few years later, failing to get a place on another long voyage of discovery, he made on his own account a visit to Iceland, again with a scientific retinue, and brought back much of interest—including the lava that Forsyth used for his rockery in the Chelsea Apothecaries' Garden.

At the exceptionally early age of thirty-five, Banks became president of the Royal Society—a body more associated with age and book-learning than youth and adventure. His election, which proved a fortunate choice for the Society, came about in an odd way, and one that is an early instance of science becoming mixed up with politics. When a powder magazine was struck by lightning, the Society became involved in an argument about which was the best form of lightning conductor; should it be one ending in a knob or one in a fork? Sides were taken, though it was generally held that the forked type was better. This was supported by the early authority on lightning, Benjamin Franklin. At that time the American Declaration of Independence was only a year or two old; Franklin was, of course, an eminent American diplomat. George III and those of his persuasion not unnaturally held anything American—particularly if it related to the protection of his gunpowder magazines—suspect. If a president of the Society strongly favouring the forked conductor held office (as seemed likely), the support of George III and his court, a matter of some weight, might be withdrawn. Banks was a naturalist and botanist of eminence, well placed in royal circles, a man of affairs, and outside the lightning conductor dispute. Diplomatically, and as it proved, wisely, the crisis was solved by his election as president. This position he held from 1778 to 1820, an exceptionally long term of office, and one during which, since they were the president's chief interest, botany and horticulture had, we may say, a position of priority in learned circles.

He became, indeed, something of a dictator. "Peter Pindar", a satirist of the time, had no liking either for science or Banks, and mocked his dominating personality:

> Blest with a phiz, he bids the members tremble;
>   To death-like silence turns the direst din . . .
> Dare members sleep, a set of snoring Goths,
> While Blagdon reads a chapter upon moths,
>   Down goes the hammer, clothed with thunder:
> Up spring the snorers, half without their wigs;
> Old greybeards grave, and smock-faced prigs,
>   With all-wide jaws displaying signs of wonder . . .

Banks, as we have seen earlier, was also the unofficial director of the budding botanical garden at Kew. So no wonder that he was asked to the meeting at Hatchard's.

Apart from his great administrative work in directing botany and scientific horticulture in its early pioneering and formative days, Banks lives today in his reputation as a pioneer in the exploration of the Australian continent, commemorated in the name Botany Bay and in *Banksia*, an important genus of Australian trees and shrubs. The Royal Horticultural Society, too, perpetuates his memory by an award named the Banksian Medal.

With Banks and the others at this meeting of the R.H.S. was Salisbury, one who devoted himself to the science of botany and the practice of horticulture. The first is exemplified by the true story of how, when in late middle age, he climbed each day for a fortnight to the top of a tall pine tree to study the details of its flowering and pollination. The second is proved by the large number of rare and difficult plants he is recorded to have grown successfully, often for the first time. But there is no doubt also that he was rather quarrelsome, and certainly did not gladly suffer those that he considered fools. He was born at Leeds, the son of a cloth merchant, Richard Markham, and was christened Richard Anthony. His mother was a descendant of an Elizabethan botanist, Henry Lyte. As a schoolboy, he was already displaying his ardour both as a botanist and gardener, being flogged, he tells us, for breaking school bounds to visit an acquaintance in order to name a plant—a form of the little "Angels' Tears" daffodil, *Narcissus triandrus* (see illustration)—which he was propagating. It was as Markham that he entered Edinburgh University, where he met and became very friendly with another eminent botanist, later to be knighted, James Smith, who was slightly his elder. Shortly after leaving the University he changed his name, having, he said, received £10,000 from an elderly woman relative so that he might be enabled to proceed with his botanical studies, on condition that he took her name of Salisbury. Soon after, the fame of his garden at Chapel Allerton, near Leeds, began to spread beyond Yorkshire. His skill in raising unknown and difficult plants prompted Banks and others to send him seeds of all that was new and rare; he was generous in distributing the plants that he raised. His botanical studies, too, brought him into correspondence with many eminent scientists both in Britain and Europe.

He then married, and after the birth of a daughter something happened quite out of keeping with the usual character of an assiduous botanist. His wife left him, taking their child. It seems that the story of his change of name and the rich relative was an invention, and that he was, in fact, heavily in debt.

However, he raised enough money to come south and buy a house and garden at Mill Hill, at that time a village in the country near Hendon. The place had belonged to Peter Collinson, a London Quaker and a successful linen-draper. He was "a great lover of animated nature in all its forms"; as an old man he declared that the plants in his garden furnished his greatest source of happiness. And a wonderful lot of plants they were. Collinson was the first gardener in the country to grow azaleas (the American kinds), kalmias and a number of other trees and shrubs now well known. He died in 1768, and when Salisbury took over the garden in 1800 he reaped the benefit of the trees that the draper had planted—chestnuts, magnolias, rare pines, cedars and cypresses—now

Plant breeding: daffodils found wild are mostly small and delicate flowers such as our native "Lent Lily" (*left*) and "Angels' Tears" (*right*). From these various species, however, man has produced a host of handsome large-flowered hybrids. Such is "Beersheba" (*centre*)

grown into fine specimens. But his immediate predecessor in the house was not interested in rare plants, and most had disappeared in the devastation. Some, however, remained. We can imagine Salisbury's excitement when one of Collinson's rare orchis or crocus made an unexpected appearance.

In his years at Mill Hill Salisbury continued collecting and experimenting with and cultivating all the new plants that were arriving from overseas. He was a pioneer in the cultivation of dahlias, in which little interest was shown for some years after their introduction from Mexico—no one at first realising the enormous possibilities of a plant now universally grown in such variety.

Salisbury carefully recorded much that he found out, writing invaluable papers in which he combined his botanical knowledge with the practical wisdom of a gardener. He was no mean artist, either, and drew many of the figures illustrating his notes. He was probably the most outstanding botanist and the most skilful cultivator of ornamental plants present at the meeting. Later, when the Society was formed, and at times seemed inclined to devote a preponderance of its activities towards the study of vegetables and fruit, Salisbury was there to urge the merits of botany and ornamental plants. For a time, too, he acted as its honorary secretary—but, like some of his successors, devoted too little time to office work, with the result that affairs got in a muddle.

He was aptly honoured in the botanical name given to an odd and interesting tree, the maidenhair tree or ginkgo from China. His friend Sir James Smith called this *Salisburia*. But under the laws which govern the names of plants, it has had to be replaced by *Ginkgo*, which is a confused and, in fact, meaningless adaptation of a Chinese name.

It is perhaps worth adding that Salisbury eventually sold his property to the committee then forming Mill Hill School. Although the house in which he and Collinson lived has disappeared, some of their trees remain.

It was probably Banks who interested his friend the aristocratic Charles Greville in science, or as it was then called, "natural philosophy". Greville was the second son of the eighth Baron Brooke, the first of the Grevilles to hold the ancient title of Earl of Warwick. He is generally put into history books—if, indeed, he enters them at all—in an unflattering light because of his connection with Miss Lyon, later to become Lady Hamilton, the wife of his rich uncle Sir William Hamilton, and Nelson's Emma. But in fact he has quite different claims, apart from his attendance at this meeting, to his own small place in history. All his life, though never a rich man and sometimes quite hard up, he worked disinterestedly for scientific progress. There was as well his pioneering work in the development of Milford Haven docks. The land belonged to his rich uncle Sir William Hamilton, who was an ambassador, much overseas, and to whom it was of little consequence. Greville, who looked after his uncle's affairs, saw the possibilities of the situation. Although Hamilton could make neither head nor tail of what his nephew was doing, he trusted him completely, and the docks took shape.

Greville was probably best known as a collector of and authority on minerals. At his death the nation bought his specimens for £13,000. But it is as a gardener that we must consider him. He first had a little garden in Edgware, which goes down in history as the first place in this country at which American blight (or woolly aphis) was noted on an apple tree. This was by his friend Banks in 1791. Later, he moved to a house near Paddington Green with a larger garden. Here, it is recorded by Sir James Smith, "the rarest and most curious plants, from various climates, were cultivated with peculiar success." As can be seen from the engravings and notes in contemporary botanical publications, Greville was indeed peculiarly successful: rare plants that he was the first to bring to flower in this country provide the subjects for several. Their names give us a clue to the nature of his interest in horticulture: camellias, tree paeonies, magnolias, hibiscus, gladiolus—all plants of great beauty. We realise, too, the jewel-like qualities of the gems and minerals that he collected, and indeed of Emily Lyon. We may regard Greville as representing the whole class of artists and connoisseurs at this meeting.

Turning to our next subject, we can say without doubt that he represented the honoured trade of nurserymen. James Dickson had a seed shop in Covent Garden and perhaps a nursery garden at Croydon as well. He was another Scot, born in Peeblesshire, where as a boy he worked in the gardens of the Earl of Traquhair. While there, it is said, his interest in botany was aroused by one boy asking another the name of that plantain which, quite unlike the plantain that grows in our lawns, has divided leaves like the antlers of a deer. "Buckshorn plantain", was the prompt answer. This surprised Dickson and he decided to learn the names of plants himself; so successful was he that at the time of the R.H.S. meeting he was an outstanding authority on mosses.

As a youth he came to London and worked in a nursery which then occupied the district upon which the Albert Hall now stands. This was then a very old and famous establishment with a long history. It is mentioned by John Evelyn as having the largest assembly of plants in the kingdom and in later times was owned by the partnership of London and Wise—the same Henry Wise who designed the gardens at Melbourne. Once again Joseph Banks comes upon the scene. The gardener employed at the British Museum was unsatisfactory. Banks, with his usual energy, went into the whole matter. He concluded that the gardens could not only be improved, but that they could be kept in a much better manner than formerly at a smaller cost. He obtained an estimate for the work from Dickson, which was accepted, and Dickson (who had not many years before opened his own seed shop) remained to his death responsible for the British Museum gardens. No doubt the position helped him to gain many of his influential customers.

He made several botanical excursions, particularly to parts of Scotland which were then quite outlandish and involved some hardship. He was an acute observer, Sir James Smith once referring to him as "the lynx-eyed Dickson".

But it is as businessman and nurseryman, and one specialising in rare and choice vegetables, that we now consider him, for on the formation of the Society he became particularly active in its affairs, for long being one of the vice-presidents.

He died at the good age of eighty-four, and "by his own wish was buried in a churchyard among the Surrey Hills where he had been accustomed to gather rare mosses." The exact place was not known until quite recently, when the assistant secretary of the Society which Dickson helped to form found it to be All Saints Church at Sanderstead.

*   *   *

The seventh member of the company at the bookshop was another gardener, William Townsend Aiton, and the only one present who could speak for the profession of garden designers, though he had now ceased this work and had become Royal Gardener at Kew on the death of William Aiton the first. He inherited his father's good qualities, and, being much in favour with the royal household, was in every way a desirable man to have at the foundation meeting.

Aiton the younger had been born at Kew, as a youth was assistant to his father at Kew, and in his later years had the arduous task of maintaining Kew Gardens after royal interest had been withdrawn from them, and at Kew he died. There were, however, two interludes in this long association with Kew. For some time before he returned there as successor to his father, he engaged in laying out gardens for several notable patrons, including the Duke of Kent, father of Queen Victoria. Later in life, after the Prince Regent came to the throne as George IV, Aiton again designed gardens for two of his royal master's building schemes—the fantastic Pavilion at Brighton and the alterations at Windsor Castle.

But at the time of this meeting things were still going well at Kew. We can imagine Aiton having a few words with Sir Joseph Banks about the young man on his staff who was now visiting the China ports to collect what plants he could find. This man, William Kerr, had just sent Banks bulbs of a new lily. These had been given to Aiton. When they flowered, England saw the tiger-lily for the first time. Aiton at once realised what a good thing it was and set about propagating the bulbs. Within a few years he had given away over ten thousand plants—a generous man and a fine gardener to whom we should give a thought when the apricot flowers of this lovely lily open in the late summer.

CHAPTER 8

The Pioneer Plant Collectors

PROBLEMS FOR PIONEERS

We have noted several occasions when botanists and travellers collected plants on their journeys and brought them safely back to England. Sometimes a plant thrived in its new home. Two early introductions were examples of this—the artichoke and, most important of all, the potato, which was later to have far-reaching effects in Europe following the discovery that it could be grown on sandy land unsuitable for other food crops.

The distribution of plants over the world is controlled by climate and geography. Eucalyptus trees grow quite well in a number of places in the British Isles. That is because the climate of those places—particularly the minimum temperature—keeps within a certain range, a range which compares with the climate of Australia where they grow as "natives". The term "native" brings in the geographical factor. During the whole period of history in which the differing kinds of eucalyptus have evolved, the Australian continent was isolated by the sea so effectively that the seeds of eucalyptus have never been able to escape to the outer world; hence eucalyptus is a native only of the Australian continent. There are, however, many other places remote from that region with climates that suit its growth (which is extremely rapid, so making the tree valuable) even better than the British Isles.

And in these places thousands of eucalyptus thrive today, having been taken there and planted by man.

At one time the British Isles were part of the continent of Europe. In those days plants and trees which were not unlike many foreign kinds grew here. Then followed an age when ice spread over most of the country; and this was followed by a warmer spell when plants gradually worked their way back from the parts of Europe that had never been frozen. A change in the surface of the land caused the sea to sweep gradually around, and the result is that the number of our native plants is quite small, restricted to those from the mainland of Europe that had a chance to get here before the land-bridge was washed away.

As an example, the only truly native evergreen trees in Britain are Scots pine, yew, holly and box, though the last is usually only a shrub. Austrian and Corsican pines, common spruce, the common silver and Douglas firs, cedars, all often seen here, were introduced from overseas. From this we realise that the British climate is such that it suits plants growing so far apart as Australia, North and South America, and Tibet.

Although a few plants had been brought here from time to time during the earlier years of our civilisation, it was not until Elizabethan times that travellers began to bring home foreign plants regularly. When the Horticultural Society was formed in 1804, only a few of the many plants and trees introduced from abroad and now common in our gardens and woodlands were to be found here.

We can see the reasons for this. Plants from remote districts with temperate climates similar to ours might have to be transported in a leisurely manner through tropical climates and on long sea voyages that would kill them, however carefully they were packed. Seeds were easier, but even today, with air transport, the hazards of collection may prevent success. For example, seed may be wanted of a rare Alpine growing in a remote Tibetan gorge. First the collection must identify the plant when it is in flower; months later another visit is needed when the seed pod is ready for collection—a few days' delay and all the seed may be spilled; then the harvest must be packed expertly and brought home.

At the beginning of the last century, when the first large-scale attempts at collection were made, the difficulties were far greater than today. It was becoming apparent to botanists and gardeners, and to none more than the enthusiastic Fellows of the new Horticultural Society, that there was an abundance of trees, flowers, fruits and vegetables that would thrive in our gardens and glasshouses if they could be safely brought here. European traders were going further afield. The North American continent was being opened—a virgin country. Trade was shortly to increase with China and Japan, countries with ancient civilisations where for centuries the people had cultivated and improved many of the plants growing wild within their boundaries. There were, too, South Africa (where Francis Masson had already been collecting for Kew Gardens), India and many other districts which had mountain ranges with hardier plants likely to thrive in cooler lands. North America, China and Japan were the richest hunting grounds for collectors.

But from our point of view, the most important contact with China in the early days was through the French Society of Jesus. One of their missionaries, Father Pierre d'Incarville, was probably the first trained botanist to work and collect in the country, where he lived from 1740 to 1756, principally in Pekin.

The handicaps under which he worked were enormous. One November day in 1751 he wrote to the secretary of the Royal Society describing them. "We are very much confin'd," he says, "we have not even the liberty of going where we please by ourselves to see things; nor can we, with prudence, believe the reports of the Chinese . . ."

And so it always has been with that great and secret country, with a break now and then for a few years until the barrier drops again. But Father d'Incarville managed to send seeds of a good number of plants that were new to the West. Some he sent on the caravans to St. Petersburg, some to Paris and many to Philip Miller at Chelsea. Possibly his best-known introduction is the Tree of Heaven, or *Ailanthus,* which is often planted in parks and large gardens on account of its handsome large leaves.

During the seventeenth and eighteenth centuries Japan had barred foreigners even more rigorously than China. All that was known of the country and its people came through the trading posts of the Dutch East India Company, beyond whose confines it was almost impossible for Europeans to step. Two scientists had, however, visited these Dutch footholds and from them studied and written about Japan as far as they were able. The first was a German, Englebert Kaempfer, who wrote his *History of Japan* at the end of the seventeenth century.

Kaempfer tells us that every house had its garden—a neatly walled-in square, with a back door, if the place be of any consequence; or "if there be not room enough for a garden, they have at least an old ingrafted plum, cherry, or apricock tree. The older, the more crooked and monstrous the tree is, the greater value they put upon it." He writes of the tubs filled with water "wherein they commonly keep some gold or silver fish as they call them, being fish with gold or silver coloured tails alive", and of their tiny rock-gardens with their dwarf trees contrived according to the rules of art.

The other traveller was a Swede, C. P. Thunberg, who made his visit nearly a century later; it was he who first found and described the now well-known *Berberis thunbergii*.

In the early part of the nineteenth century, while Japan's barriers were still up, we came to know a good deal more of the people and natural history of the country through the remarkable activities of Philipp von Siebold.

Siebold, the son of a Bavarian doctor, was born in 1796. His portrait shows a fierce, beetling-browed, bearded face surmounting a challenging figure dressed in uniform.

Siebold graduated as an eye specialist, and was appointed physician-naturalist to the Dutch East India Company. He went to the Dutch foothold on the island of Deshima, off Nagasaki, from which they traded with the mainland under difficult and restricted circumstances. The Japanese, it seems, were very prone to eye-troubles, which they had not the skill to cure. Siebold took advantage of this and by bartering his services, which were greatly in demand, secured quite unusual privileges and freedom of movement even on the mainland. He was then able to study and collect the remarkable plants which the Japanese grew in their gardens. (He studied and wrote on the general natural history of Japan, too, with important results.) He visited the capital, Tokyo (then called Yedo), and there made a large collection of plants; even more remarkable, he persuaded the Imperial Astronomer to give him a map of Japan. This was a document of high secrecy and of great interest to the Western world. Unfortunately, while sailing back to Deshima, his boat was wrecked, and soldiers spotted the map. Japanese heads were lopped off and Siebold was sentenced to two years' confinement on his island, to be followed by banishment. This seems not to have interrupted his studies and collecting, however, for in 1830 he sailed for Holland with a grand collection of 485 plants. These were lodged at Antwerp until Siebold quarrelled with the authorities there, upon which he moved them to Ghent Botanical Gardens. At this moment, the war which resulted in the independence of Belgium from Holland broke out. Siebold had to leave Ghent; and his plants were confiscated and distributed among the members of the already famed nursery trade in Ghent. His new azaleas and camellias in particular proved of great value to the growers—though Siebold eventually got some back.

During the following years he was concerned with several organisations with high-sounding names, often supported by funds from the public (one even had royal support for a time). They were all, however, no more than commercial plant-importing and nursery businesses run by Siebold, using his great knowledge of and connections with Japan solely for his own advantage; for a time he even secured a monopoly in the Japanese plant trade.

In 1859 Japan was in a state of turmoil and anti-European feeling was intense. It was thought that Siebold's presence and prestige as a doctor would help to stabilise the position and tend to stop the murders of Europeans, which were embarrassing to the authorities. So out he was sent, this time by the Dutch government. The Japanese gave him a palace of his own. Before long he was in a key position, able to ignore the Japanese and Dutch alike, and behaving as a petty dictator. Eventually the government managed to get him back to Holland by a trick. On his return Siebold, finding that he had been duped, severed his connection with Holland and returned to his native Germany, where he died in 1866.

We can overlook the behaviour of this extraordinary man when we find how it is counterbalanced by his scientific work—his study of Japanese animals, of the Japanese language, of Japanese plants epitomised in the classic *Flora Japonica* (compiled jointly with a German, J. G. Zuccarini, and exquisitely illustrated by unknown Japanese artists) and the hundreds of plants that he brought to Europe.

Primula sieboldii, a popular plant in Japanese gardens, named in honour
of Philipp von Siebold

Enough has been shown of the difficulties placed by nature and man alike in the way of the plant-hunter at the beginning of an era which was to prove one of the most important in the history of plant introduction. We can now balance against them an ingenious invention.

Nathaniel Ward was a doctor, a self-sacrificing man who lived and practised in Welclose Square not far from the London Docks. In spite of the grimy surroundings of his home, he was an ardent naturalist. One day he brought back a chrysalis from the country. Wishing to keep it and hatch it out, he took a glass jar into which he put some soil and then buried the chrysalis in it. The container was almost air-tight. Before long he noticed that seeds in the earth were germinating, and growing happily, forming plants that would normally not have lived in the warm and smoky atmosphere of an East-end house. Basing a series of experiments on this observation, in 1833 he evolved the Wardian case, a contraption made from sheet metal and glass, almost air-tight, in which it was possible to keep and grow plants whatever the surrounding atmosphere. The device was soon used to make fern-cases in which ferns—lovers of moist and humid conditions—could be grown in dry, smoke-filled, stuffy drawing-rooms.

Dr. Ward's case was, however, to prove far more important in transporting the plant-hunter's trophies across seas and continents. His invention made possible the first introduction of tea to India, of quinine-producing plants from the New World to the Old, and the first cultivation of bananas outside China.

EAST OF THE PACIFIC: DOUGLAS IN NORTH AMERICA

In the last decade of the eighteenth century several journeys of exploration were made to the Pacific coast of North America. The most important was the voyage of the *Discovery* under George Vancouver—who had served under Captain Cook and was imbued with the same fine and generous spirit. He had taken with him Dr. Archibald Menzies, R.N., as naturalist. Menzies' account of what he saw, particularly in New Albion, later to be known as California, painstakingly recorded, gave a tantalising picture of the plants that grew there. Descriptions of forests of trees, taller than any known in Europe, a rich variety of shrubs and herbs, all in a climate not dissimilar to that of the British Isles, excited the more enthusiastic gardeners and planters.

The secretary of the Horticultural Society, Joseph Sabine, was perhaps the most enthusiastic and energetic of them all; no doubt he wished that the Society should have the honour of first cultivating some of these newly described plants in the garden that had just been established at Chiswick. (Sabine was so keen on developing this garden that he neglected his office work, relying on an assistant, who, though he is said to have read the minutes of meetings in a very fine style, embezzled the Society's funds. Sabine eventually had to resign in consequence.)

The Society was busy making plans to send a collector to North America when, in 1823, Dr. W. J. Hooker, then director of the Glasgow Botanic Gardens, whose work at Kew has been described, recommended to Sabine a Scotsman of twenty-five named David Douglas as suitable for the job.

Douglas was born near Perth, the son of a stonemason. As a boy he showed an unusual love of natural history. When about eleven years old he became apprenticed as a gardener and at nineteen entered the service of Sir Robert Preston of Valleyfield on the Forth. Sir Robert had a good botanical library and a head-gardener who appreciated the worth of his new assistant. Douglas was given access to the books, and made profitable use of this privilege. Two years later he was again fortunate, gaining a post at Glasgow Botanic Gardens while Hooker was still its head. His character attracted the professor, who was then engaged on a Flora of Scotland. He took the young man with him on several botanising trips into the remote Highlands, and Douglas profited from the incomparable fund of knowledge and experience that was Hooker's. Backed by Hooker's and other weighty recommendations, and no doubt after being impressed by Douglas himself, the Horticultural Society appointed him to explore and collect seeds, as well as to procure pressed specimens, of trees and plants not then in cultivation.

His first trip was to the Eastern United States. As with all his travels, he kept a journal from the moment he set out—in this

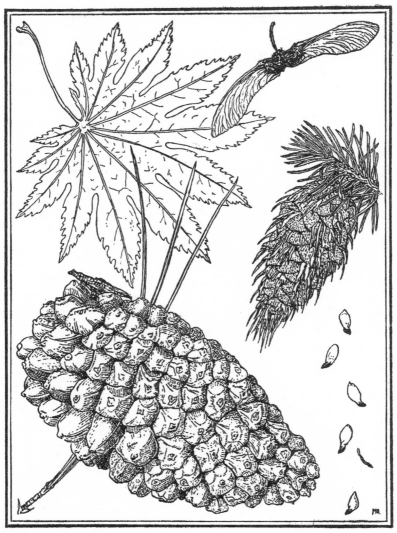

Plants introduced by David Douglas from North-West America: *top*, vine maple; *left*, Monterey pine; *right*, Douglas fir

case it begins when he leaves London, including even the journey
to Liverpool (whence he set sail in May 1823), with details noted of
the gardens and plants that he saw while on it. His main object seems
to have been to study the many oaks growing in the Eastern States.
It was known that several American oaks grew much more quickly
than our own, though subsequently experience has shown that few of
them really thrive in the British Isles. He also reported on the gardens
and garden plants that he found. For instance, Mr. van Ransaleer of
Albany had, he wrote, "a large space of ground occupied as a pleasure
or flower garden, which is a novelty in America, as little attention is
paid to anything but what brings money or luxury for the table." And
he wrote of Mr. Jesse Bull that his garden was large and "all divided
by hedges of hawthorn from Britain. Hedging is a thing unknown in
a general sense."

This trip was soon over, and seems to have been little more than
a reconnaisance of the vast continent in which the fame of Douglas
still shines.

It was on the 26th July, 1824, that he next sailed, this time from
Gravesend, for the North Pacific coast of America, for what was
to prove a historic journey. He had spent the time since his return
in studying the records of the voyages of Vancouver, had examined
Menzies' specimens, and made himself as familiar as possible with all
that he was likely to find. The surgeon on his ship, the *William and Ann*,
was Dr. John Scouler, M. D., an even younger Scotsman than Douglas,
for he was scarcely yet twenty. He too was an enthusiastic naturalist and
adventurer; they were firm friends. Scouler's name is commemorated
in the small lilac-flowered shrubby *Penstemon scouleri*, which may
be found in rock-gardens, and which Douglas introduced later from
North America.

The journey to Columbia took about eight and a half months. The
boat had to sail round Cape Horn and the length of the coasts of South
and North America before reaching the mouth of the Columbia River.
Sailing up it to the small trading post of Fort Vancouver (not the
same place as today's city of that name), Douglas saw for the first
time the huge forest trees, flowering shrubs and rich variety of plants
with which he had already familiarised himself from books and dried
specimens.

Soon he was at work, travelling sometimes with another white companion, often only with a native guide. Before long he was suffering hardships, which are recounted unemotionally in his journal.

In the early pages we come to this account of an adventure at the well-named Cape Foulweather. This he faced with a Mr. Alexander McKenzie, for they had sent the Indian porters who were accompanying them home, for the good reason that otherwise they would have starved.

> "The wind", he writes, "about midnight increased to a hurricane with sleet and hail, and twice were we obliged to shift our camp, the sea rising so unusually high. We had no protection save what a few pine branches and our wet blankets afforded, and no food ... We walked along the sandy beach sixteen miles to Whitbey Harbour, where we found the village deserted, our prospect not in the least bettered. We remained here several days, faring scantily on roots of *Sagittaria saggitifolia* and *Lupinus littoralis*, called in the Chenook tongue *Somuchtan*, and from continual exposure to the cold and the want of proper sustenance I became greatly reduced."

The hardships of this trip were suffered in vain, for the berries they had collected for seed had later to be eaten as food, and most of the specimens they had gathered were discarded as there was no one to carry them.

A page or so later he records triumphantly that he was allowed to embark on an expedition in a small canoe with two reams of the special paper used to press and dry specimens—though to do so it was necessary to leave behind most of the small supply of clothing that he would otherwise have taken.

That these hardships were worth while can be realised from the exultation of his description of a view near the Grand Rapids:

> "The scenery ... is grand beyond description; the high mountains in the neighbourhood, which are for the most part covered with pines of several species, some of which grow to

an enormous size, are all loaded with snow; the rainbow from
the vapour of the agitated waters, which rushes with furious
rapidity over shattered rocks and deep caverns, producing an
agreeable although at the same time a somewhat melancholy
echo through the thick wooded valley; the reflections from
the snow on the mountains, together with the vivid green of
the gigantic pines, form a contrast of rural grandeur that can
scarcely be surpassed."

And we catch the feeling of excitement as he describes a night spent
on a rock, this time alone with still another Scot, a Mr. McLeod, unable
to pitch a tent because of the steep slope. Vigilance was necessary,
he says, for they were surrounded by 450 savages "inclined to be
troublesome". A few wax tapers remaining, Douglas wrote letters and
pressed mosses through the night. In the morning the "troublesome"
Indians came close, and "accidentally" splashed water on the gunlocks
of the white men. Mr. McLeod was pushing through them to get to his
boat when Douglas saw that an Indian was covering him with his bow
charged with an arrow. Quickly Douglas raised his gun, charged with
buck-shot, covered the Indian, and dared him to shoot. At that moment
a powerful and friendly chief arrived on the scene—and all was peace.
This chieftain was, Douglas records, the finest figure of man that he
had ever seen, 6 feet 6 inches high. Friendship between the two was
sealed by the "Grass Man" (as Douglas was called) taking a drilled
shilling from his pocket and with a piece of brass wire hanging it in
the hole made through the chief's nose.

Then there was the night of 25th October, 1826, "one of the most
dreadful I have ever witnessed". At that time he was entirely on his
own except for his horses, with food stores so low that he was able to
afford but one meal a day. The teeming rain, driven by the gale, made
a fire impossible; at midnight his tent blew down, so he lay rolled in
it and a wet blanket in the bracken.

"Sleep of course was not to be had; every ten or fifteen
minutes immense trees falling, producing a crash as if the
earth was cleaving asunder, which with the thunder peal on
peal before the echo of the former died away, and the lightning

in zigzag and forked flashes, had on my mind a sensation more than I can ever give vent to . . . My poor horses were unable to endure the violence of the storm without craving of me protection, which they did by hanging their heads over me and neighing."

Douglas was particularly excited by his discovery of the Sugar Pine (*Pinus lambertiana*), with huge cones, more than a foot long, hanging from their points like the sugar loaves that used then to be seen in grocers' shops. This tree is the tallest pine in the world—and the cones are only formed at the top. Douglas naturally wanted seeds to send home, and quite early on in his travels he had collected a number of cones, which, however, had to be left behind when he was forced to escape from hostile savages.

In 1826 he again came upon a group of "this most beautiful and immensely large tree." One, thrown by the wind, was 215 feet long. High up on the others hung the "sugar cones". Taking his gun, he was shooting them down. The noise attracted eight Indians from out of the woods. They were painted with red earth, carried bows and arrows, spears made of bone and flint knives. They sat down—and prepared their weapons.

There was no chance of escape. Douglas covered them with his gun, and after some argument, promised them tobacco if they would collect him more cones. Off they went—and Douglas slipped back into the woods. That night he recorded the adventure, adding, "Not a book to read, constant expectation of attack . . . I am now lying on the grass with my gun beside me, writing by the light of my Columbian candle—namely, a piece of wood containing rosin."

The following day his guide was attacked by a bear . . . But we have seen enough of the man now for it to be almost unnecessary to add that the Horticultural Society of London duly received from him seeds of the Sugar Pine—a tree, unfortunately, that has not been very successful in the British Isles, although such a favourite with Douglas. Its name commemorates Aylmer Bourke Lambert, at that time a great authority on conifers. Douglas wrote amusingly to Scouler: "What would Dr. Hooker do to dine under its shade, Mr. Lambert could not eat anything if he saw it."

Until the spring of 1827 he worked only to the west of the Rockies. Much of the ground near the coast and around the Columbia River was impossible for horses; canoeing and walking were the only methods of getting about. Yet, by April, when he reached the Rockies to cross them on his trans-continental journey to the east, over seven thousand miles of travel lay to his credit.

On the journey he met other famous travellers, among them the botanist Thomas Drummond, in honour of whom *Phlox drummondii** is named, who was botanising on the eastern side of the Rockies. He also encountered John Franklin, coming back from a pioneering voyage in the Polar Sea, who was eventually to lose his life seeking the North-West Passage.

Throughout this journey Douglas, who had always been keenly interested in birds of prey, had with him a live eagle captured in the Rockies, intended for the London Zoological Society; but after surviving the two-thousand-mile journey, it met with a fatal accident at Fort York, which was a small port on the banks of Hudson's Bay from which the Hudson Bay Company's boats, loaded with furs, set sail for England.

It was from here that Douglas sailed on 15th September, 1827, an exhausted and rather sick man, his eyesight failing after an attack of snow-blindness, but triumphant in the almost unbelievable success of his mission.

The voyage seems to have restored his health. On arrival in London, the Scottish stonemason's son found himself famous. Learned societies elected him to their membership; and the doors of famous houses opened to receive him as an honoured guest. He worked on his journals and notes, and published several papers on the trees and plants that he had seen. The trip had accounted for the introduction of 164 species, many of which are now often to be found growing in our woodlands and gardens.

His stay in England was not long, however. On 26th October, 1829, he sailed once more for the Pacific coast and the Columbia River. The voyage was broken by a month's stay in the Hawaiian Islands.

---

* This plant had later to be reintroduced to American gardens from England, so rare was it in its home.

We know rather less of this second period of exploration, for towards its end, during a daring journey down the Fraser River, the light canoe in which he travelled was smashed to pieces on some rocky islets. Douglas and his party were lucky to escape with their lives; his journal, his equipment and a collection of 400 plants were lost. Fortunately he was an excellent correspondent, and letters to Hooker, Sabine and others had already told much of what he did and found. It was at the beginning of this journey that an episode occurred which throws a light on his generous character. We have noted earlier that Sabine was such an enthusiastic gardener that he neglected his office work as secretary of the Horticultural Society, with the result that his assistant embezzled the funds. When this was discovered, Sabine, who was nominally responsible, naturally resigned. Hearing of this Douglas concluded that Sabine, his staunch friend and supporter, had been slighted and at once severed his own connection with the Society. Fortunately, however, he continued to send them his plants and seeds, which were shared with his friend Hooker at Glasgow.

On this trip he added the work of a geographer and astronomer to that of plant collector. During his stay in England Joseph Sabine's brother, later to become General Sir Edward Sabine, F.R.S., trained him in surveying. He was also helped by the Colonial Office. Douglas can claim, therefore, to be not only a pioneer in the study of plant life in North America, but also one of its pioneer surveyors. We are told that subsequent surveys have confirmed the accuracy of his work.

On this journey, too, he moved south and paid a long visit to California, working from Monterey. Here he found a wealth of previously unknown plants. In one letter home he tells of finding nineteen or twenty new genera and 340 new species. It was while here that he became the first botanist to see and describe the giant Redwood growing in its native land.

It was after this Californian interlude, on his return to Vancouver, that Douglas set out to explore the northernmost and least accessible area that he had yet attempted—the trip that was to end so disastrously in the Fraser River and therefore about which we know little.

In the autumn of 1833 he was back in California. A letter he wrote on 11th November of that year from his "tent on the hill of Yerba Buena" to one of the many friends he made in California still exists.

On the site where he pitched his tent there now stands the city of San Francisco.

A few days after, he sailed for the Hawaiian Islands. Here he climbed mountains and volcanoes; he wrote of the active crater of one volcano, which he reached after being deserted by all but one of his servants: "One day there, is worth one year of common existence." After his arduous and disappointing last trip in North America, he was having a magnificent time, which is vividly and fully described in his journal and letters. But it was not to be for long.

Captain Vancouver had introduced cattle to the islands, which had become wild. The natives dug pits into which these fell. On 12th July, 1834, the mangled body of Douglas was found in one of these traps, crushed by a savage bullock.

One of the greatest of modern American botanists, Dr. Charles Sprague Sargent, said of him that no other collector reaped such a harvest in America or associated his name with so many useful plants.

There can be little doubt that the most important of his introductions were the dense and prickly Sitka spruce, the Douglas fir (*Pseudotsuga taxifolia*) and the Monterey pine (*Pinus radiata or insignis*). The first has been planted in huge numbers in Scotland and Wales. The second, with its fragrant foliage and pointed beech-like buds and tassel-like cones, is now a familiar and valued tree in our woods. The Monterey pine, found wild only in a very small area of California, is well known here as an ornamental tree, also used as a wind-break, in the milder parts of the British Isles—recognised by its three-needled leaves and the large cones remaining for years clustered round the branches. It is in places like New Zealand, Australia and parts of South Africa, however, that this tree has become of importance. There, in a milder climate than our own, it grows at an extraordinarily fast rate and quickly provides large quantities of useful timber.

In our shrubberies and woodlands we owe to Douglas the handsome-foliaged common mahonia (or berberis), with its yellow flowers and fruit like tiny grapes, and the snowberry or *Symphoricarpos*. Both have now become naturalised in Britain.

Other shrubs he introduced are the flowering currant *Ribes sanguineum*; *Garrya* with its long tassel-like flowers, opening in winter; and the vine maple, *Acer circinatum*.

We owe to him also musk—which has lost its scent since he brought it over—clarkia, the little blue nemophila, and *Lupinus polyphyllus* from which our modern lupins have been evolved. It would, indeed, be difficult to find a garden which did not include one of the many plants that he introduced. When we add to the pleasure that his garden plants have given to millions of people the economic value of his other introductions, the usefulness of his geographical surveys and the value of his observations on and specimens of animals and birds, we do not hesitate to place him among the greatest of the pioneers.

The story of Douglas can only be told through those who have studied his vivacious letters to the many friends that he attracted, and the journals that survived his journeys. These are, of course, scattered about the place and for the most part have not been printed. There is no doubt that he had intended writing a full account of his travels, adventures and discoveries, but volumes that would certainly have been among the classics of travel and adventure remain unwritten.

WEST OF THE PACIFIC: FORTUNE IN CHINA AND JAPAN

China, for botanists, was in almost every respect the opposite to North America. It was a densely populated land with an ancient civilisation. The arts, and the cultivation of plants in particular, had been practised for centuries. In the early part of the nineteenth century China was in a particularly bad state of internal confusion, and trading through those few ports used by the Western traders became almost impossible. An English army was sent to change the situation. As a result, in 1842 the Treaty of Nanking was concluded, which gave Britain increased powers of access to the mainland of China, defined British rights in the ports, and gained the island of Hong Kong.

By that time John Lindley, professor of botany at University College, London, was assistant secretary of the Horticultural Society, having succeeded the man who under Sabine embezzled its funds. Lindley was the son of a nurseryman at Catton in Norfolk. As a boy, he dreamed of becoming a plant collector; once his parents found that he was sleeping on the floor and not in his bed—to harden himself, he assured them,

for the arduous life that he was to lead. Quite early in his career
he had attracted the attention of Sir Joseph Banks, and became an
assistant in Banks' library—whence he progressed to lifelong service
of the Society and a professorship, for which he was better suited than
the adventurous career of his boyhood dreams.

The signing of the treaty rightly seemed to him and other Fellows
of the Society an opportunity to send a collector to China. Lindley
approached the Government department concerned with a request
for help. The civil servants of the day adopted their traditional
well-meaning but obstructive attitude, and did little more than point
out the difficulties involved, suggesting that nothing should be done
until the new British consuls had taken up their positions in China.

The Society, however, had among its Fellows a certain John Reeves,
recently retired from the important post of Inspector of Tea at Canton
for the Honourable East India Company. Reeves was an ardent amateur
botanist and enthusiastic gardener. During nearly twenty years that he
spent in China he had corresponded with men like Banks, Sabine and
Lindley. He had arranged for native artists to live in his house and,
under his supervision, make accurate paintings of wild and garden
plants. (The Royal Horticultural Society and the British Museum now
have many of these.) More important, he was one of the first men
to arrange for the despatch of live plants in a systematic manner in
charge of the captains of the East Indiamen. He saw that to do this
successfully it was first necessary to get the plants well established in
pots and then to take the greatest care in packing and transporting
them. The captains caught his enthusiasm and vied with one another
in bringing their charges home to England in a thriving state.

John Reeves now became the leading member of a committee formed
by the Society which determined to engage a collector and despatch
him to China without waiting longer for the consent of Her Majesty's
officials.

Robert Fortune, the new superintendent of the hothouse department
of the Society's garden at Chiswick, was the man chosen. Like Douglas
a Scot, he was born at Kelloe, Berwickshire, on 16th September, 1812.
He had made his own way up the ladder to Chiswick in much the same
way as Douglas, though not through Glasgow Botanic Gardens, but
the even more famous Royal Botanic Garden at Edinburgh.

Japanese anemones: the first of the so-called Japanese anemones were
introduced to Europe by Robert Fortune

The brilliant character and personality of Douglas seem to have been replaced in Fortune by quieter, less emotional and, from his writings, almost impersonal qualities. The courage, integrity and persistence in adversity of the two men were certainly comparable; Fortune, too, in a different manner made friends wherever he went and was most successful in managing the Chinese. It is surprising that the Society was so successful in choosing a man who, though he had never been overseas, was well able to cope with the unpredictable situations that he encountered.

It was, perhaps, his lack of experience and the fact that he was untried which resulted in the voluminous and detailed instructions which were issued to him before he sailed. Prior to that, he had some arguments with the committee about how he was to carry out the work. One concerned firearms. The committee considered that a stout stick would be all that was required to defend himself in a brawl. Fortune answered that possibly this would be so in the treaty ports known to them, where the forces of law and order were near to hand, but pointed out that a stick would be little use in dealing with an armed Chinaman should he be able to travel into the interior. He got his gun.

An interesting departure was that Fortune was to take with him some of the new Wardian cases filled with growing plants. His purpose was to observe the effects of the voyage on the plants in the cases, and later to distribute their contents as presents. He also carried a stock of vegetable seeds with the same ends in view. The cases were, of course, to be refilled by his own collections on the voyage home.

To read the instructions now is to realise how little the committee knew of China apart from the few trading ports. After going into minute detail on every conceivable point, there generally follows the qualification that Fortune should use his discretion. He was, however, particularly asked to seek certain plants—some of them mythical—such as the peaches of Pekin, cultivated in the Emperor's garden and weighing two pounds each; those shrubs that yield tea of different quality; the double yellow roses, "of which two kinds are said to grow in Chinese gardens"; the plant which furnishes rice-paper; paeonies with blue flowers ("the existence of which, however, is doubtful"); camellias with yellow flowers ("if such exist"); the lilies of Fokien, eaten as chestnuts when boiled; the azalea from

Lou-fou-shan, a mountain in the province of Canton; and cocoons of the Atlas moth called Teen-tsam from the same place.

These pages of instructions are endorsed simply at the end with "Accepted, Robert Fortune."

On 26th February, 1843, he sailed in the *Emu* on this pioneering journey to China, the fabulous land of Cathay.

This is how he described his arrival:

"On the sixth of July, 1843, after a passage of four months from England, I had the first view of the shores of China; and although I had often heard of the bare and unproductive hills of this celebrated country, I certainly was not prepared to find them so barren as they really are. Viewed from the sea, they had everywhere a scorched appearance, with rocks of granite and red clay showing all over their surface: the trees are few, and stunted in their growth, being perfectly useless for anything but firewood. A kind of fir-tree (*Pinus sinensis*) seems to struggle hard for existence . . . but is merely a stunted bush . . . Was this, then, the 'flowery land', the land of camellias, azaleas and roses, of which I had heard so much in England?"

His opinion of the people was equally unflattering:

"This country has been long looked upon as a kind of fairy-land by the nations of the Western world. Its position on the globe is so remote that few—at least in former days—had an opportunity of seeing and judging for themselves; and besides, those few were confined within the most narrow limits at Canton and Macao, the very outskirts of the kingdom, and far removed from the central parts or the seat of the government. Even the Embassies of Lord Macartney, although they went as far as the capital, were so fettered and watched by the jealous Chinese that they saw little more than their friends who remained at Canton. Under these circumstances much that was gleaned from the Chinese themselves relating to their country, was of the most exaggerated description, if not entirely fabulous. They from the highest Mandarin down to the meanest beggar are filled with the most conceited notions of their own importance and power; and fancy that no people, however civilised, and no country, however powerful, are for one moment to be compared with them."

Then soon after landing:

"It was now my lot to be seized with that dreadful fever ... I lay in a very precarious state for several days, without the means of procuring medical aid; but the sea air probably did more for me than anything else, and, under Providence, was the means of saving my life."

In spite of this inauspicious beginning, Fortune was soon getting about the place (he first worked from Hong Kong), ingratiating himself with, and gaining the confidence of, the mandarins with fine gardens and nurserymen with stocks of plants unknown in this country.

He describes his first visit to a mandarin with all its weight of formality and etiquette—and how the mandarin was much more anxious to impress him with a very ordinary telescope which he thought to be unique than to show him round the garden.

Fortune had some trouble with the nurserymen at first. So interested was he in their stocks that they became alarmed as to his intentions, and set watch-boys to warn them when he approached, so that their gardens might be barred against him. He was soon able to persuade them, however, that he too was a man of business and would pay for all he took.

Faced with all the bewildering variety of plants displayed by these nurseries and gardens, Fortune showed a remarkable gift for selecting only those plants which would do well and be popular in British gardens, and it is to this that we can attribute the fact that most of what he introduced are still among our best and most highly prized garden plants.

He was often in tight corners. Once, to his fury, the attackers sent his plants flying in all directions. At another time he was set upon by thieves, who were after his silk neck-cloth, which they coveted as a headdress.

Fortune sailed to the island of Chusan several times, and here at last he was to see the native flora of temperate China—the treasure-house from which the gardens and nurseries that he had hitherto seen were supplied:

> "Almost all the species of a tropical character have disappeared, and in their places we find others related to those found in temperate climates in other parts of the world. I here met, for the first time, the beautiful Wisteria wild on the hills, where it climbs among the hedges and on trees, and its flowering branches hang in graceful festoons by the sides of the narrow roads which lead over the mountains. The *Ficus nitida*, so common around all the houses and temples in the south, is here unknown; and many of those beautiful flowering genera, which are only found on the tops of the mountains in the south, have here chosen less exalted situations. I alude more particularly to the azaleas which abound on the hillsides of this island. Most people have seen and admired the beautiful azaleas which are brought to the Chiswick fêtes [the early flower shows of the Horticultural Society], and which, as individual specimens, surpass in most instances those which grow and bloom on their native hills; but few can form any idea of the gorgeous and striking beauty of these azalea-clad mountains, where, on every side, as far as our vision extends, the eye rests on masses of flowers of dazzling brightness and surpassing beauty. Nor is it the azalea alone which claims our admiration; clematises, and a hundred others, mingle their flowers with them, and make us confess that China is indeed the 'central flowery land'."

On these sailing trips his boat was more than once attacked by pirates: prompt use of the gun that he was so nearly denied saved both his life and his plants.

We are most interested in the garden plants that he collected on this stay in China, during which he also worked around Shanghai, but it is important to notice that he gave the first detailed account of the cultivation and manufacture of tea in China, and a great deal of valuable and interesting information about other matters such as artificial incubation of ducks, irrigation systems, ploughs and other aspects of Chinese life such as their culture of chrysanthemums, and fireworks. He wrote in detail of the dwarfed trees in the gardens of the mandarins:

> ". . . they contain a choice selection of the ornamental trees and shrubs of China, and generally a considerable number of dwarf trees. Many of the latter are really curious, and afford another example of the patience and ingenuity of this people. Some of the specimens are only a few inches high, and yet seem hoary with age. Not only are they trained to represent old trees in miniature, but some are made to resemble the fashionable pagodas of the country, and others different kinds of animals, among which the deer seems to be the favourite. Junipers are generally chosen for the latter pupose, as they can be more readily bent into the desired form; the eyes and tongue are added afterwards, and the representation altogether is really good. One of the Mandarins of Ning-po, anxious, I suppose, to confer some mark of favour upon me, presented me with one of these animals—plants I should say;—but as it was of no real use to me and as my collections of other things were large, I was obliged to decline the present, which he evidently considered of great value, and no doubt wondered at my want of taste."

He was particularly interested in the Chinese cemeteries, so unlike anything in Europe, and of the use of plants for their decoration:

> "The flowers which the Chinese plant on their tombs are simple and beautiful in their kind. No expensive camellias, moutans, or others of the finer ornaments of the garden, are chosen for this purpose. Sometimes the conical mound of earth—when the grave is of this kind—is crowned with a large plant of fine, tall, waving grass. At Ning-po wild roses are planted, which soon spread themselves over the grave, and, when their flowers expand in Spring, cover it with a sheet of

pure white. At Shanghae a pretty bulbous plant, a species of *Lycoris*, covers the graves in Autumn with masses of brilliant purple. When I first discovered the *Anemone japonica*, it was in full flower among the graves of the natives, which are found in the ramparts of Shanghae; it blooms in November, when other flowers have gone by, and is a most appropriate ornament to the last resting-place of the dead."

It was when on a solitary exploration of a graveyard lying among remote hills that courage and quick action saved his life. He suddenly realised that a group of Chinese present were crowding round him with but one purpose, robbery, and perhaps murder. Without warning, he suddenly hit out and, surprised as they were, sent them rolling down a slope. Those remaining pulled him down, but he struggled free, dragging and fighting them to the door, which their colleagues outside were trying to bolt. But Fortune's prompt action forestalled them, and his weight thrown against it before the bolts slid into place not only burst open the door but sent the men outside sprawling. Struggling free, he ran as fast as he could, though a thrown brick hit him in the back and injured him; but the robbers had clearly had enough, and Fortune was soon back in safety.

After three years of what he called "wandering" but which was in fact a period of continuous collection and observation of trees, shrubs and plants, both wild and cultivated, combined with the compilation of a mass of information about the practically unknown habits and conditions of the Chinese, Fortune set sail for home.

His narrative ends:

"After a long but favourable voyage, we anchored in the Thames on the 6th of May, 1846 . . . and at the present time (October 20, 1846) *Anemone japonica* is in full bloom in the garden of the Society at Chiswick, as luxuriant and beautiful as it ever grew on the graves of the Chinese, near the ramparts of Shanghae."

On his return, he was appointed Curator of the Chelsea Physic Garden.

In 1848 he was off to China again, but now on a different quest. This time he went for the East India Company to try to collect the tea plant, so that the tea industry, then a monopoly of China, might be established in India. This was an exceptionally difficult task, as naturally the Chinese had no wish to part with their seeds or secrets of preparation. But Fortune, using the Wardian cases, succeeded. In 1852 he made a further visit connected with the tea industry. He ranks, therefore, as the pioneer of the great tea industry in India—though subsequently the descendants of his tea plants were replaced by kinds more suited to Indian conditions which were brought from Assam.

In addition, he collected a number of valuable new garden plants on these "tea" trips.

His success as collector can be measured if we name but a few of the plants that he introduced now to be found in practically every garden. Perhaps the most famous is the winter-flowering yellow jasmine, one of the hardiest and gayest of all plants. This was at first considered tender and grown in a greenhouse. Then there is the rose-coloured weigela (or diervilla)—from which numerous garden forms have been raised—first seen by Fortune in the gardens of a mandarin on Chusan Island. The list includes, too, a forsythia, notable as one parent of the hybrid usually grown in our gardens, and quite often itself seen; one of the most popular of ornamental conifers, *Cryptomeria japonica*; a number of important rhododendrons, azaleas and tree paeonies; the lyre-flower or bleeding heart, *Dicentra spectabilis*; the handsome-leaved and sweetly-scented winter-flowering *Mahonia bealei*; *Prunus triloba*, with its tight little double pink flowers in spring; and, of course, the first form of the Japanese anemone, which with its pink or white and other garden forms subsequently raised or introduced is such a feature of our gardens at the end of summer. He brought, too, the ancestors of the pompon chrysanthemum.

Those are but a few of the plants that Fortune sent to England from China during his three journeys.

Not content with this, he set off again in 1860, this time with Japan as one of his objectives. He probably financed this trip himself, as the profits from successful plant introductions and also from the volumes that he wrote about his travels must have been appreciable.

If Siebold was the real pioneer in Japan, Fortune and, it should be added, John Gould Veitch,* who was also there in 1860, run him close.

In spite of Siebold, Fortune had little idea of the nature of the country; he had read of cataclysmic earthquakes, the miraculous powers of the Emperor, salamanders . . . "I had", he wrote, "long looked upon Japan much in the same light as the Romans regarded our own isles in the days of the ancient Britons."

But on his arrival off Nagasaki, so well known to Siebold, he found a bay dotted with little islands and exactly like a Chinese garden magnified until it was life-size.

From Japan, which he observed and of which he wrote with his usual care, he brought some of the first Japanese chrysanthemums, the extraordinary umbrella pine, or *Sciadopitys*, the double deutzia, and finally:

> "The plant remarkable above all others which were met at this time, for its great beauty, was a new primrose (*Primula japonica*). I shall never forget the morning on which a basketful of this charming plant was first brought to my door. Its flowers, of a rich magenta colour, were arranged in tiers, one above another, on a spike nearly two feet in height. It was beyond all question the most beautiful species of the genus to which it belongs, and will I doubt not, henceforth take its place as the 'Queen' of Primroses."

Fortune returned to England on 2nd January, 1862. He settled down quietly, living mostly in Kensington until his death in 1880—one of the small number of plant collectors to achieve the peace and leisure of a long and placid retirement. Occasionally he wrote articles for the gardening press, and was sometimes to be seen at horticultural functions. Perhaps in spite of his modesty, he would then reflect that he had done more than any man to bring the glories of Cathay to British gardens.

---

* Veitch forestalled Fortune by a few weeks in introducing the "Golden Rayed Lily", *Lilium auratum*. But he was not a collector of the stature of Fortune.

CHAPTER 9

The Makers of New Plants

THOMAS ANDREW KNIGHT

The story of the pioneers of plant-breeding is an odd and interesting one. First, we shall take a man representative of others widely known and influential, making experiment after experiment, often with successful results, but failing to grasp the simple principles to which his work should have led him. Then, a few years later, another man, living a quiet and unknown life, discovers these principles and even publishes them—yet, although many eminent scientists and gardeners were by now studying and practising plant-breeding in a hit-and-miss manner, these discoveries were for long disregarded.

The first of these two was a great and important figure among the pioneers of our modern countryside, but it was as a gardener specialising in the cultivation of fruit and vegetables that he was pre-eminent.

Thomas Andrew Knight began his long and useful life in 1759. There is a fine portrait of him, painted in middle age. We see a country squire, quietly dressed in dark clothes relieved by a spotless white cloth at his neck. A high, domed forehead rises above a face with a complexion ruddy from the sun and breezy showers of the Welsh Marches. Every feature shows balance and integrity. The eyes look out keenly, rather quizzically; not much, we are sure, passes by them unobserved. It is a wise face, too; a multitude of the doings of men, animals and plants have not only been seen but patiently understood.

He was the second son of a clergyman who inherited wealth and large estates in that favoured and fertile part of England where Shropshire and Herefordshire join, not far from the changeless town of Ludlow. This fortune came from ancestors who had developed the iron industry round Madeley in Shropshire. Today, when we pass through that desolate and ravaged district, and see the barren slag banks, the only relic left now behind after the rich minerals were exhausted, it is some consolation to recall that the wealth won from it was later put back into the land elsewhere, not only by Thomas Andrew Knight but by his cousin Frederic, who used his share to reclaim much of Exmoor from a wilderness.

Thomas first went to school at Ludlow, his mother by then being a widow. Finally, he went up to Balliol College, Oxford. There his career was not successful in the usually accepted sense. Much of his time was spent wandering round the countryside with a gun under his arm and a dog at his heels. He was profitably studying nature at first hand instead of the classics at second.

During vacations he often stopped with his brother, Richard Payne Knight, who was nine years older, with a London house in Whitehall. Richard was in every way the opposite to Thomas. His interests lay in the works of man rather than nature. Art, and in particular the antiquities of Greece and Rome, were his chosen subjects. He was, as we have seen elsewhere, interested in gardens, but only in their design—favouring the romantic and picturesque styles which at the time were unfashionable. He was then using some of his fortune in building a big house at Downton, near the banks of a suitably picturesque gorge on the River Teme. It was an extraordinary place—the outside taking the form of a baronial castle in accordance with his delight in romance, the inside being designed after the classical manner suitably to display his collections of Greek and Roman antiquities!

This interesting and wealthy bachelor had a wide circle of friends, whom he entertained at his London house. This was an important matter for Thomas, for while visiting his brother at Whitehall he came to know the members of the brilliant intellectual society of the day, whom he would otherwise never have encountered at his quiet

Herefordshire home. It was in that county, never far away from the River Teme, then, as now,

> The country for easy livers,
> The quietest under the sun

that Thomas spent the rest of his long life on coming down from Oxford. At first living with his mother, he continued his patient and persistent observations of nature, and began a series of horticultural and agricultural experiments that continued for half a century.

In 1795 Sir Joseph Banks with his electrifying enthusiasm makes another of his entries into this history. In that year Thomas met him when at Richard's London house. Banks was at once impressed by the young Herefordshire squire, now becoming an experienced farmer, and well embarked upon those experiments which his riches and estates enabled him to conduct on a large scale. The impact of Banks upon Knight was even more important. From now on, he began recording in full the details of all his many experiments. This he did at first largely in the form of long letters to Banks, who replied to his young friend with comments on the results in which were embodied the fruits of his extensive knowledge of natural history, accompanied by generous encouragement given with all the authority of the President of the Royal Society. Later, Knight made his work public in many papers presented to the Royal Society and the newly-formed Horticultural Society, of which he was an original member.

Although the correspondence with Banks covers observations on all sorts of subjects, the first related to that which was uppermost in all his studies—experiments in plant-breeding, with details of experiments that he had made in crossing peas.

Whereas the Leicestershire farmer Robert Bakewell had already made great progress in producing improved strains of sheep and cattle, little had been done to improve plants. Knight's pioneer experiments in this line were brought about by an original line of thought. Herefordshire from early times has been the home of fruit-growing. The trees were increased by grafting. The chosen kinds had been selected from those very rare chance seedlings that were an improvement on existing fruits. The act of grafting means that the tree resulting is not an entirely new tree, as in a seedling, but a bit from an old tree joined up with the root of a young tree. It is the bit of the old tree that develops, and from it, in turn, another graft may be taken.

Thomas Knight rightly thought that a great many trees in the Herefordshire orchards were poor trees, bearing small and miserable apples. He looked round and observed many very aged apple trees withering away and dying. Seedlings, though their fruit was poor, were vigorous. The next step was a realisation that the newly grafted tree, in itself probably produced from an older grafted tree, was not, as it seemed, a young tree, but a very ancient tree kept alive by the young roots to which it had been attached by man. That, he concluded, was the reason why the quality of so much fruit was bad—it was due to the decline of the trees owing to the oncoming of old age.

This ingenious theory is now generally held to be wrong. But it caused Knight to set about doing something to put things right. What I must do, he said to himself, is to try to produce a succession of *entirely* new trees producing good fruit—that is, trees raised from seed—which will keep up a steady supply of vigorous stock. And I must do this by purposely mating two trees with good qualities, by placing the pollen of one on the stigma of another, and selecting the best of their children.

On these lines Knight spent a lifetime of work. He raised many fine new kinds, not only of fruit trees but of many other plants. By trial and error he accumulated a mass of valuable information, and his example encouraged others to experiment. He failed to discover the correct scientific principles underlying the breeding of plants and animals, but even without them produced good results. And here we may take note of a rather extraordinary fact. Today, while scientists seem to know all the facts about plant-breeding, very few of them are able to produce the required results. It is still left to practical men of the type of Knight who, making use of the work of scientists, have the necessary patience and powers of observation combined with a sort of instinct to produce our new flowers and fruit.

Many of Knight's productions became widely known and grown— some are living even now. He gave them delightful names, and to quote a few will give us an idea of the wide range of his experiments. Of apples, we have Spring Grove Codlin, Downton Lemon Pippin and Herefordshire Gillyflower; cherries were Elton (named from the home where he went to live upon his marriage), Waterloo (which first fruited just before that battle) and Black Eagle; strawberries, Elton and Downton (again after his two homes); pears, Winter Cressane and Belmont. And equally delightfully named were the nectarines, plums and red currants that he raised from seed and propagated.

I do not know whether anyone has properly studied the many papers that he published, or even counted their number. Besides those on plant-breeding, others embody his studies and experiments on the ascent and descent of sap in trees, the movement of tendrils in plants, on mildew and on the construction of greenhouses. The methods of cultivation of the Guernsey lily, celery, strawberries and many other plants and vegetables were all studied and generally improved after they had received his attention. Indeed, Thomas Knight's horticultural experiments would seem to be a full and valuable life's work on their own; certainly, through them alone he would rank as a pioneer.

Yet, in addition, he played a full and exemplary part in the daily life of his time. In 1791 on his marriage he went to live at Elton Hall, which, as we have seen, gave its name to some of his productions. The house still stands, and possibly in its grounds remain some of the trees that Knight planted. Some years later, he moved to his brother's home, Downton Castle, and took over the management of the big estate that went with it. Richard Payne Knight was always happier in town among the company of philosophers, artists and writers. He had, too, by now spent much of his fortune on the sham castle with its superb collection of antiques—later to become part of the British Museum. Richard therefore relinquished his country home and its ten thousand acres to his brother, and henceforth lived in London.

Thomas managed the big estate personally without interrupting the steady flow of experiments. He was an enlightened landlord and improved the condition of his tenants. He worked on the improvement of his stock, and raised a very hardy and successful breed of sheep. His energies were devoted to many activities in his loved county of Hereford—particularly towards raising the general standard of farming. He was elected a Fellow of the Royal Society. He was President of the Horticultural Society from 1811 until 1838. He met a dreadful blow with courage—the death of his only and loved son in a shooting accident; his sorrow was counteracted by an even greater devotion to his experiments.

He seldom moved far from his native place; those rich acres and lovely hills between the Wye and the Teme provided for him a big enough world, a kingdom of never-ending interest.

As his years increased, only an annual visit was made to London. This was to give his presidential address to the Horticultural Society, the body with which he had closer ties than any other. In 1838 he travelled to London for the annual meeting. The long coach journey was too much for him and he became ill. On a day in May he died, far from the blossoming Teme-side orchards, but no doubt content in the knowledge that the exhibition of the society over which he had presided for twenty-seven years was considered the best ever held.

Thomas Andrew Knight stands today as a pioneer of the practical adaptation of scientific methods to horticulture, and particularly to the extremely important work of plant-breeding. This craft of producing something better by intent and not waiting for one of the rare chances of nature is surely one of the latest and greatest achievements of man. During most of his life Europe was at war, and politicians squabbled even more ingloriously than is usual. Their names, and those of generals and battles, filled the news sheets of the day and still clutter our history books. But who can doubt that the work of the quiet Herefordshire squire has benefited mankind far more than savage battles, and that his fame is of a more worthy kind than that of the noisy politicians?

JOHAN MENDEL

The practical results of the work done by Thomas Knight and those who followed him were important. Yet for long afterwards no one understood the causes that lay behind the effect; Charles Darwin's theory of the origin of species was not introduced with scientific proof until long after Knight's death, though during Knight's lifetime Darwin's grandfather, Erasmus, had guessed at it pretty correctly. Yet the Darwinian theories, important as they were, did not explain the problems that puzzled plant and animal breeders. They worked in darkness and ignorance, occasionally producing excellent results by following rule-of-thumb methods, and entirely without understanding of what they were doing.

The immensely important discovery of the scientific principles upon which the breeding of plants and of the animal kingdom depended was eventually made by Gregor Johan Mendel, Abbot of Brunn (or Brno), a rather remote town in Central Europe. In every way, his life and work were in contrast to those of Knight. He lived for the most part in comparative poverty. His discoveries were made in a tiny little garden. He published little about his work. His one epoch-making paper reporting his achievements was duly read before an insignificant local society, printed, put away unnoticed by the world, forgotten . . . and then triumphantly discovered—after his death.

This priest, gardener, amateur scientist and pioneer was born on a July day in 1822. You are unlikely to find his birthplace on a map; it was a small village of some seventy houses called Heinzendorf, roughly at the point where Poland, Germany and Czechoslovakia meet. It was quite a prosperous little place, the inhabitants making their living either from their lime-kilns or by farming—for, as in Knight's Herefordshire, the land was fertile; gardening and fruit-growing were popular occupations. Mendel's family had lived in the place for many generations, none of them, it seems, ever very rich or very poor. The name is found in the old records among magistrates, burgomasters and parish councillors. The village is among mountains and Johan grew up to be of typical short, sturdy mountain stock. He was baptised Johan only—Gregor was added when he joined the Augustinian order of monks.

The Mendel family were traditionally keen gardeners. Johan's father had a smallholding, with a rich and well-tended orchard. From his early days the boy helped with this. Gardening was to remain his lifelong hobby; so much so that when he retired, fruit-growing and beekeeping became once again his main interests in life.

Johan was immensely fortunate in the village of his birth. The influential lady of the manor, encouraged by the enthusiasm of the local pastor, saw to it that natural history and elementary science were taught in the school. This was quite exceptional at that time, and indeed the authorities frowned upon it as likely to undermine the religious faith of the village children.

As he grew up, Johan's life became difficult. He wished to study philosophy. This meant an expensive education. To pay for it, he needed to take private pupils. These were not forthcoming in sufficient numbers. Overwork and worry over this soon caused a breakdown in his health. Recovering, he decided that the best life, and one in which he could most happily follow his studious inclinations, was to be found by joining the Augustinian brotherhood. This he was permitted to do, and in 1843 went to the monastery of St. Thomas at Brunn. Once more he was fortunate, for its prelate, Cyrill Franz Napp, was a man "pulsating with physical and intellectual energy". Napp made Brunn and its monastery a home of learning and enterprising thought and experiment.

Gregor Mendel, as he now became, was happy among his new surroundings. But in the years that followed, he had several ups and downs. He planned to become a highschool teacher to bring him an income sufficient to maintain himself. Though today his is one of the most famous names in the history of natural history, it was in this subject that he failed in the qualifying examination! There was, however, a good reason: his education till then had been on the whole rather haphazard, and the proper university training which was really necessary had always been beyond his reach. Then there is a story that to raise money he entered for the state lotteries, which induced him to study the laws governing his chances of success—a branch of mathematics which he was later to use with important results in his experiments.

At last he achieved his ambition, went to the University of Vienna and was able to become a popular and much loved member of the staff at Brunn Modern School.

Then, in 1856, using the little strip of garden in the monastery of St. Thomas, he began—in his spare time—the researches which long afterwards made him famous.

Nine years later, on a February evening, Father Gregor Mendel walked to give a talk to the Brunn Society for the Study of Natural Science. It was called *Experiments in Plant Hybridisation*. In it were described the results of these experiments. They had consisted in crossing different strains of peas and hawkweeds. No doubt his hearers enjoyed the talk, for he was a popular master at the local school, and the subject was certainly quite interesting. At a later meeting he gave another talk. Perhaps this had its origins in the studies that he had made of the laws of chance in the days when his hopes had seemed to depend on winning a lottery prize, for it concerned some mathematical aspects of his plant-breeding experiments. As a talk this was apparently judged a failure. The audience could not see what possible connection permutations and combinations might have with botany.

The outside world of science, apart from one or two acquaintances with whom Mendel corresponded, remained in ignorance of these papers. Their immense importance—which indeed Mendel himself at first did not fully grasp—remained, therefore, unknown. Surprisingly, Mendel never corresponded with Charles Darwin, whose studies of the origin of species were well known to him. If he had done so, Darwin might have seen the significance of Mendel's work. In any event it would then have become known beyond a limited circle. A quarter of a century's time would not have been wasted by eminent scientists who were seeking for what already was to be found in the archives of the humble little scientific society at Brunn.

In 1874 Mendel put his scientific work on one side. His working hours were henceforth devoted to the service of his religious order, and his energies to certain intricate financial matters concerning the taxation of monasteries. He became Abbot of Brunn, remained keenly interested in science, but in his last years gave all his spare time to his orchard and his bees.

In 1884 he died. He was mourned as a man admired and loved by his fellows, particularly those who had been his pupils, and as an able servant of his faith and monastery. Perhaps a few words were said about his interest in science—but to the great and growing world of science and scientists, where his fame now belongs, he remained unknown and therefore unmourned.

He is remembered for his discovery of the simple principles of the laws of inheritance—the laws that govern with a horrifying severity and inevitability certain characteristics in the make-up and character of a plant, or bird, of man himself. These characteristics and qualities are transmitted by complex means from generation to generation, sometimes one of the most marked disappearing from the surface for a generation or more, but always lying hidden away ready to come up again according to law—the law that Mendel discovered. We must be clear about one thing: Mendel did not discover the reasons *why* these things happened—he discovered the laws that govern what *does* happen; and his discoveries related to the laws in their simplest, elementary form.

We have seen the vast range of Thomas Andrew Knight's experiments, which, though they gave a multitude of results, merely bemused the seeker for their underlying causes. Possibly Mendel knew something of this work. He certainly knew of the experiments of Darwin's cousin, Galton, who had simplified his field somewhat and studied only the breeding of basset-hounds. Mendel was far from the hubbub of scientists. For generations his had been simple people; he himself lived simply among his fellow-monks. He saw the vast and elaborate field over which his fellow-searchers had or were ranging: Knight with his ten thousand acres on which to experiment, Galton with his complex breeding of basset-hounds—and others like them. Mendel chose the common wild pea as the subject for his experiments. It has certain peculiarities (which, incidentally, Knight had noticed and experimented with years ago).

There are several different strains with easily recognised features. For instance, one is tall, another dwarf. When the seeds of the dwarf kind are sown, only dwarf plants come up. The same is true of the tall kind: it produces tall-growing seedlings only. Again, some have coloured flowers, some have white. Some have smooth skins, some wrinkled. All these different strains are reproduced exactly from their seed, or, as we say, breed true. The reason for this is that each flower is fertilised and seed produced only by its own pollen. Insects do not visit and therefore do not "cross", or hybridise, the flowers of the different strains.

Mendel, however, realised that he could do what in nature never happened. It was easy for him to get some pollen from a coloured flower and put it on the stigma of a white flower. Then the seed on the white-flowered plant would have as father a coloured-flowered plant.

On his little plot, he was therefore able to carry out experiments, selecting and crossing peas with only two differing qualities, and reduce his possible "permutations and combinations" accordingly. He really worked in the opposite way to his fellow-experimenters.

One can take an example, flower colour white and pink, and see what he did.

He took a plant with a white flower and "crossed" it, as we have described above, with the pollen of a pink flower. A pod of seeds was set on the white plant. He sowed them to see what would happen. The seedlings came up and within a month or two flowered. All had pink flowers. At the same time, he reversed the parentage. He put the pollen of a white flower on the stigma of a pink flower; now it was the pink flower which bore the seed which he sowed. The result was the same—all pink flowers.

Something important is already learned: it does not matter which plant bears the seed, white or pink, the result is the same.

The next step is to allow the pink children born of crossed pink and white parents to set their own seeds as in nature.

He now has a lot more seedlings to examine. The result is rather surprising: they are of two kinds—one with pink flowers, the other with white flowers. The seedlings are just like the plants with which we started; none are halfway between. The next interesting thing to notice is that for each white-flowered plant there are three pink-flowered.

Mendel called the pink-flowered strain, which forms all the first generation and a three-to-one majority of the second, the *dominant* of the two simple factors with which he was dealing. The white, which disappears for a generation, he called *recessive*.

Each time he repeated his experiments the results were the same; he was therefore beginning to discover what he sought—*laws*.

Mendel now allowed his latest generation to set their own seed again. These were sown. The seedlings of the white-flowered plants all came true. The seedlings of the pink-flowered plants were mostly pink with a small number of white. The proportions of each continued to be regular, always more pink than white, and including a majority of pinks that produced only pinks. Repeating the experiments, the results and the proportions of pink to white remained constant.

Mendel carried out many more experiments, but we have seen enough to get an idea of what he was discovering. He did not discover *what* caused the pinkness and whiteness, but by tracking the *results* of these causes through successive generations and analysing them mathematically, he was able to show that they were carried along from generation to generation, sometimes secretly, and would make themselves apparent according to predictable mathematical laws.

Later, he carried his experiments to a much more advanced stage, using hawkweeds as well as peas. As we have seen, the account of them, and the laws deduced from their results, were placed before his fellow-scientists at Brunn. And then having done this, he turned his attention elsewhere—to the affairs of his church, to his orchard, to his bees. Truly a man as simple as his experiments and little concerned with worldly fame.

Meanwhile, other scientists were getting more and more involved and confused in their attempts to find these rules. Countless experiments were made and the results were recorded. Rabbits, pigeons and orchids were being crossed and bred, crossed and bred. The details of the reproductive cells were studied and knowledge of them greatly increased. Darwin's theory of evolution was generally accepted. But no one could find the master key that would open the door disclosing the pattern underlying the laws of inheritance. It was as if men had discovered by experiment that twice two are four and twice nine are eighteen but could not discover the principles of arithmetic that gave the intermediate stages.

Then, in 1900, three scientists, ransacking the scientific literature of the world, seeking in the most unlikely places—even among the archives of the remote little Brunn Society for the Study of Natural History—unearthed the paper that Father Mendel had read on that February evening years before.

The key to the problem was found. A garden-loving abbot had forged it, of common materials in a small workshop. He rattled it about in the lock for a bit to make sure that it worked—then put it away.

It is pleasant to learn that the Royal Horticultural Society was the first to arrange for the translation of Mendel's paper into English. International conferences that the Society organised also played an important part in the development of this new branch of learning. At one of them, indeed, the name of "genetics" was first used—and that is what the science is now called. It is a science that has helped in producing not only such flowers as our modern roses and daffodils (see illustration on page 94), but vastly improved strains of our staple food-yielding plants.

CHAPTER 10

The Eminent Victorians

The gardens discussed so far have been of two kinds. We have seen the gardens of the great: the earlier ones formal and ornate, with their extravagant waterworks and statuary; then, later, the man-made landscapes. The other gardens have been much smaller—the hobbies of "curious gentlemen" or those with inquiring minds, and of botanists.

Little has been said about the middling class of garden—the sort of garden that most of us have today. The reason, of course, is quite simple—the big middle class of today is a product of comparatively recent times; it developed enormously during the great Victorian age. During that period thousand upon thousand of medium-sized houses with medium-sized gardens were built by prospering tradesmen, engineers and professional men. These people were keen and intelligent, and prepared to improve their position by reading and learning; they created a demand for gardening magazines such as had never existed before, as well as for books about horticulture. Improvements in engineering, developments in science, and an increasing number of new plants from abroad were all welcomed by this new class. In the magazines of the day, for instance, one finds that their houses and small estates are always described as "private residences", while the old homes of the nobility remain "seats". As the years passed the number of "residences" increased rapidly, while the "seats" slowly diminished.

The changed conditions brought about a new type of garden—which we can call Victorian. The large new body of gardeners were at first without leadership and without much tradition. This was, however, soon provided by a new type of teacher—that of gardener-journalists and gardener-editors.

As today we look back on those years during which the ever-changing Georgian scene was transformed to the steady and increasingly prosperous era of Victoria's reign, there is little difficulty in seeing who were the dominating figures in this new class—the men who led the new age of gardening, during which science and horticulture became allied as never before.

MR. AND MRS. LOUDON

John Claudius Loudon was born at Cambuslang, Lanarkshire, in 1783. He died in 1843, when Queen Victoria had only been on the throne for a tenth of her long reign; but his work was carried on after his death by his devoted and younger widow, and the books that he wrote and which she revised and reissued, lived on long after both were dead. They formed the foundations upon which many of the new middle-class gardens were reared.

Loudon soon showed signs of an intelligence and energy well above the average. He went to live with an uncle in Edinburgh so that he might have a full education. As a child, he was interested in gardening and science—particularly chemistry; the boy was clearly going to belong to the new scientific age then (and not now, as we often mistakenly think) being born.

He seems to have made quick progress with his schooling, and among his other qualifications developed a natural talent at drawing, becoming a capable draughtsman.

At fourteen years of age he left school to be apprenticed to a firm of nurserymen. This was at the Edinburgh branch of the already long-established firm of Robert Dickson.

The firm's principal business lay at Hassandeanburn, and it had long specialised in producing trees, and no doubt it was while training with Dickson that Loudon laid the foundation of his great knowledge of them—a subject which of all the many that he touched upon seems to have been dearest to him.

He was a superlatively industrious apprentice. During working hours he toiled at his training as a nurseryman and in landscape gardening. Out of them, he went to classes. Two whole nights a week he sat up preparing his work. In order that he might perfect his knowledge of Italian and French he paid for lessons by making translations of works written in these languages for an Edinburgh publisher. So that he might keep his familiarity with French, for many years afterwards he used it in writing his daily journal.

In 1803 Loudon came south and settled in London. His abilities, energy and knowledge soon brought him success as a journalist; in the year of his arrival his first essay, on laying out public squares, was published. Three years later his writings on botany brought the honour of election to a fellowship of the learned Linnean Society.

In that same year he was stricken with a serious illness which was to affect the course of his life. No doubt his untiring energy had exhausted his body, and rheumatic fever caught him in its grip. The first consequence was that when he recovered, one arm was permanently shortened, and he also suffered henceforth from a weakness in a knee.

The second was the result of his convalescence. He left London for the better air of Pinner in Middlesex—then, of course, far in the country. Keenly observant, he soon concluded that English farming practice was inferior to that carried on by his neighbours in Lanarkshire. As soon as he was well enough he rented Wood Farm, Pinner, and brought his father down south to join with him in managing it on the Scottish system. The venture succeeded.

In 1809 Loudon moved and rented a large farm at Tew Park in Oxfordshire. Here again he was an innovator. In addition to farming the land, he took pupils who wished to learn his up-to-date and efficient methods. He thus pioneered the modern agricultural college. This project was an even greater success. At the same time, he wrote books on farming matters—ranging from finance to instructions on laying out buildings—and in three years made a profit of £15,000. This was a big sum in those days, and we can understand that he now felt justified in selling his farm, investing his wealth, and embarking on a foreign tour to gratify his insatiable desire for knowledge.

We must pause for a moment, however, before we follow him on this journey and visit the village of Great Tew, one of the loveliest on the Oxfordshire border of the Cotswolds. It stands by Tew Park, where Loudon farmed. It owes no little of its present beauty to the skilful planting of trees, particularly evergreens. That was the work of Loudon during his short residence. And they are by no means the only trees that he planted and which now serve as his memorial.

The fortune safely (as he thought) invested, Loudon set out. His travels were planned to cover the capitals and chief towns of northern Europe—Sweden, Germany and Russia. He could not have chosen a more difficult period in which to make his journey, for he was no longer a strong and active man but handicapped by his rheumatic ailments. All went well in Sweden, but on reaching the eastern states of Germany in 1813 he found himself in the midst of the horrors of the last stages of the Napoleonic wars—when, after his retreat from Moscow, the Emperor was making a desperate effort to keep his long-oppressed enemies at bay.

The scattered villages were often as not burned out. Those still standing were crowded with refugees and wounded soldiers. War had scorched the earth of crops; the barren fields were littered with the skeletons of horses and cows bleaching in the sun. In one village he encountered a force of two thousand Russian soldiers behaving like savages. His carriage was attacked by a band of Cossacks; the coachman's courage and presence of mind saved their lives. As he moved towards Russia, wolves menaced the horses drawing the carriage. One night, sleeping in his coach outside a refugee-crowded village, starving cows ate the straw that he had spread round his feet for warmth. Under these unpleasant conditions Loudon travelled from Prussia on to Moscow, following the route taken by Napoleon in his disastrous campaign. Arrived at that once great city, he found it but a heap of smouldering ruins.

At last, the long and adventurous journey over, Loudon came home to a bitter surprise. He learned that while he had been away, the business in which he had invested his money had failed; his fortune was lost and he was now a poor man. Much of the rest of his life was spent trying to restore it. At times he met with considerable success, but in the end it became a losing struggle fought always against odds, the worst of which was ill-health. In spite of this, his energy and courage never failed him.

In debt though he sometimes was, it is nothing to the debt that gardeners still owe to him for the activities that he now undertook. His first was the production of an *Encyclopaedia of Gardening*. Nothing first-class of this sort had appeared since Miller's old *Dictionary*—now, in spite of revised editions, out of date and expensive. Besides, Loudon aimed his *Encyclopaedia* at a new target—the rapidly increasing wealthy middle classes, spending their money on newly built houses which had to have gardens. They sprang up in their hundreds, for the most part near the big towns where their owners had made their money. Possibly, therefore, one title that Loudon should carry is that of the pioneer of suburban gardening—which means pioneering the sort of garden that nearly all of us have today.

To perfect his practical acquaintance with gardens and plants of all kinds he made another tour abroad—this time to France and Italy, the sunny homes of gardening and horticulture from immemorial times.

Back in England once again, another disaster befell him. He suffered pain from the arm that was shortened consequent upon his rheumatic fever. Massage was at that time coming into fashion as a treatment for such complaints. An establishment at Brighton had achieved some reputation of success, and in 1820 Loudon went there for treatment. So crude and elementary were the methods of the day that, instead of the pain in his arm being relieved, the alleged massage broke the bone! To make matters worse, the surgeons of the day were equally incompetent. The break was so near to his shoulder that they could not set it. The pain—it was his right arm—was agonising. Yet steadily he worked on. Articles, pamphlets, books followed one another. He advised on the laying out of gardens and estates. To keep up this flow of work, something had to be done to deaden the pain. He took doses of laudanum—one of those deadly soothing drugs, once taken, desperately difficult to leave. His dose reached a wine-glassful each day—enough to undermine the will and health of most men. At last he underwent a further ordeal. The arm was amputated—in those days there was no anaesthetic. This done, his indomitable will was brought into action. Day by day he reduced his dose of laudanum. Each time he took one, he added water to the medicine bottle; at last he was taking pure water! The dread habit was broken for good.

In 1826 he staked another claim to be a pioneer. In that year he launched *The Gardener's Magazine*. This was the first cheap and successful illustrated gardening paper published for the general gardening public. "The Director", as he styled himself, brought together a team of knowledgeable contributors. The novice as well as the expert was catered for; to this day many of the articles and illustrations are of considerable interest.

Particular attention was given to the application of scientific and mechanical developments to gardening. The use of cast iron in structures such as greenhouses, and modern methods of heating them, are subjects occupying many pages. In an early issue he describes how, at the Zoological Society's garden in Regent's Park, he saw a new device at work, a *machine* to cut the grass. Until that time lawns had been scythed, or the grass just beaten down flat. It was made, he tells us, by the Phoenix Foundry at Stroud. And he had no doubt that it would be outstandingly successful! This invention of the mowing machine is typical of the changes that were coming about in Loudon's day, and to which he and his magazine gave such a welcome.

In 1828, with his usual advanced and catholic interest, he reviewed in the magazine a novel that had little enough to do with gardening. It was called *The Mummy*—a three-volume "romance of the twenty-second century". The book, now long forgotten, was no less remarkable and prophetic than the more famous works of Jules Verne and H. G. Wells. There was, for instance, a description of ploughing by means of a steam engine instead of horses. This struck "the Director" as an ingenious idea. He commended the book highly. So impressed was he by its original ideas that he made inquiries about the, to him, unknown author. A friend offered to effect an introduction. To Loudon's surprise, instead of a sophisticated, worldly-wise man, he met a girl of twenty! The result was romantic. In 1830 James Loudon married Jane Webb—for that was the name of the girl who wrote *The Mummy*. In that year, therefore, began the close partnership which justifies us from now on in referring to Mr. and Mrs. Loudon almost as one being. Indeed, Jane Webb, the high-spirited girl, disappears to become Mrs. Loudon, the most capable assistant of Mr. Loudon and one of the soundest and most popular writers on gardening, the countryside and natural history of the first half of Victoria's reign.

She was born, of quite well-to-do parents, in Birmingham. To visualise the appearance of this now sprawling giant among cities as it then was needs a good deal of imagination. Hundreds of acres that it has now grasped were then gentle midland countryside; delightful estates and gardens which then abounded have long since disappeared under row upon row of factories and streets. As may still occasionally be seen, the houses of the citizens in this lively new town showed cultivated taste. Squalor there was, but the horrid acres of Victorian slums had not yet arisen. The arts as well as the sciences prospered; the outlook of the inhabitants was much more enlightened and in advance of those in the older towns. It must have been a delightful place for a lively and intelligent girl. She travelled too. The first slim book she published of prose and verses is chiefly about a year spent wandering around the continent of Europe.

Then, while still in her teens, her mother died. The distress shattered her father's health. He too lost money heavily in the same period of bad trade as did Loudon.

The family moved to a small property, then far in the country. Jane became housekeeper, looking after her ailing father and her younger sister. Then, as now, living in the country had its drawbacks. Long afterwards she wrote of this move:

> "When my mother died, my father with a shattered constitu-
> tion and a greatly diminished fortune retired to a small estate.
> The place had a good house, commanding a splendid view. At
> first I was enchanted with the change. My first trouble was
> three gentlemen calling unexpectedly. My father asked them to
> stay to dinner. We were seven miles from the town. I shall not
> enter into the details of that well-remembered dinner . . ."

Poor Jane! Most of the rest of her life was like that, coping with difficulties, illness and at the same time writing, always writing. For *The Mummy* was, like all she wrote, designed to help finan-cially—though, of course, Jane must have had great pleasure from its writing, as the role of authoress was that to which she always aspired.

Her new house was one of those square red-brick Georgian houses set high among the Worcestershire hills. From the grounds, hills on the distant Welsh borderlands could be seen; closer, only a mile or two away, in the vales below, lay two famed gardens—Hagley and The Leasowes. (And but a little walk away she could climb and look in the other direction upon Shakespeare's distant Arden.)

We are surprised that the book she planned among these charming surroundings was not the usual romantic dream of a girl, but a horribly true forecast of the world as it is today; we have not even had to wait until the twenty-second century for it to come into being!

For in that century—in the year A.D. 2126 to be precise—England was tranquil and prosperous, ruled by a Queen. There were rumours of wars. The people are still unhappy and restless—for there are no longer any difficulties to conquer! The working classes are so well educated that they have become pedantic—the cook, Celestine, spends her time drawing Greek statues instead of the poultry.

Englishmen, now with everything that they want, still grumble about their lack of liberty. The social services are perfect; nowhere in Europe can boast such palaces as our prisons. London is a beautiful city, with wonderful gardens on either bank of the Thames; but as they are free, few people visit them. Air travel is so cheap and commonplace that really rich people prefer to stay at home. And other commonplaces of 2126 were gas-fires, coffee-machines and overhead railways. Boots and shoes were stamped out by machines. An engine was used to milk cows. Wireless and telephones were, it is true, rather simpler in their construction than those we have today—and there was, of course, the tractor-drawn plough which so intrigued the Director of *The Gardener's Magazine*, and which must bring us back now to Mr. and Mrs. Loudon.

They set up house in Porchester Terrace, Bayswater. In the small garden they grew a remarkable collection of plants. And they wrote, wrote, wrote ... always with the urgency that the lack of pounds, shillings and pence breeds, but first and foremost because they were born leaders and educators—not so much of the poor, but of the new, uprising middle-class. They believed that it was the duty of people with estates to run them properly and use the scientific methods then coming into being; above all, that every house should have a good garden, designed on common-sense lines. (Loudon's own word for good design was that it should not be formal, picturesque, or any other kind of -esque, except "gardenesque"—that is, a garden designed by a practical gardener making proper use of materials that he had at hand, as well as all the new materials being provided by science and the first plant-hunters.)

The Director of *The Gardener's Magazine* travelled widely over the British Isles. He did not spare his criticism of those gardens of the great which, he felt, did not come up to the standard that their owners should set. Stowe came in for some caustic remarks. Even more so did the extravagant garden then in the course of being laid out by the fabulously rich Earl of Shrewsbury at Alton Towers among the hills where Staffordshire and Derbyshire meet. The gardens at Alton were in fact the forerunners of what was to degenerate into Victorian extravagance, lavishness and bad taste. If the later Victorians had followed the advice of Mr. and Mrs. Loudon, much of what we tend to mock now would never have happened.

Alton, for instance, included within its confines an imitation of Stonehenge, a Chinese temple, a monument in the Greek Corinthian style, genuine ruins, imitation ruins, real caves, sham caves—none of those features designed for the Earl being thoughtful designs but imitative copies. The planting of trees and shrubs around them was equally lavish and tasteless.

Loudon, it must be admitted, did not successfully lay out many great estates himself. His outstanding work in garden design—and, with his tree-planting, his most lasting memorial—was in London's squares and gardens, so many of which were laid out during his lifetime. It was Loudon's determination that at last persuaded the authorities to improve Kensington Gardens. First, the high wall that surrounded it was pulled down and replaced by railings, so that all of London passing down Bayswater Road could see into the park with its fresh green. Flowering shrubs were planted along the walks to give privacy. Close plantations of weedy, drawn-up, ageing trees were thinned out, and where necessary new trees were planted. In what was called the "garden-ground", he arranged for the planting of flowering and rare trees. Today, when they have matured into fine specimens, giving Kensington Gardens its peculiar charm, few people, I fear, are aware that they owe this pleasure to Loudon.

We may be interested to read what the public thought about these improvements. The author Leigh Hunt thus commented on the changes that were due to Loudon's endeavours and to whom he gives credit:

> "A very agreeable and unexpected novelty was added not many years since; to wit, a considerable strip of public flower-garden. The flowers, and the trees also, are labelled with their botanic as well as popular names: and as many of both are not common, and at the same time are beautiful, not only is general information diffused, but cultivators learn what to ask for of nurserymen, and gardens in general profit accordingly.

> "It is calculated that England is now three or four times the country it used to be in regard to its show of flowers, and that the importation of foreign trees, particularly from America, has given its parks, and will ultimately give its woods and field-sides, an addition of autumn colours, very like changing its landscape from northern to southern, or from greys and dingies, to reds, oranges, and gold."

Trees and shrubs are the features of all Loudon's designs; his love of them—and, above all, of trees—was the abiding passion of his life. "In olden times, trees were the very temple of the gods," he wrote. And to that temple of trees he was to devote his greatest energies and in so doing lose another fortune.

Soon after he married, he began work on the *Arboretum et Fruticetum Brittanicum*, or *The Trees and Shrubs of Britain, Native and Foreign*. No one, before or since, has attempted to produce such an all-embracing study. Particularly as to trees, it remains unsurpassed. The eight volumes are referred to again and again by our most recent scientific writers—an immense tribute to one who was not a professionally trained scientist.

The work was planned in advance down to the smallest detail, a forerunner of one of our modern research campaigns. Lists of tabulated questions were sent out to all the great landowners and others who grew trees. The views of leading botanists and other authorities in England and overseas were obtained. References in over 2,000 books were consulted—the plays of Shakespeare, the works of the poets, the writings of travellers in all the temperate parts of the globe, the Greek and Roman classics, in addition of course to all the standard botanical literature in English, French, German and Russian, all were consulted. A standardised system was evolved for making drawings and artists were sent to work all over the country; 2,532 small figures and 364 full-page plates resulted, all produced by the slow process of wood-engraving.

The text, apart from the volumes of plates, runs to over 3,000 pages.

The *Aboretum* is titanic in conception and precise in the minutest detail. Loudon's Continental travels, his fluent knowledge of the languages used by the principal foreign botanists, and his own encyclopaedic mind all played their part in bringing together the work of his team of correspondents—he names no less than 826 of them!—and then, in his own person, welding it to make a whole. Jane, like her husband, worked day and night. Often out with him, she acted as a secretary. Her particular responsibility seems to have been collecting together and tabulating the statistics that poured in.

In the meantime, *The Gardener's Magazine* and their other activities continued.

In 1838 the eight volumes appeared. In the introduction, Loudon writes wise words which show once again his love of trees:

> "Trees are not only, in appearance, the most striking and grand objects of the vegetable creation; but, in reality, they are those which contribute the most to human comfort and improvement ... Man may live and be clothed in a savage, and even in a pastoral, state by herbaceous plants alone; but he cannot advance further; he cannot till the ground, or build houses or ships, he cannot become an agriculturalist or a merchant, without the use of trees."

Loudon's daily timetable while engaged on this undertaking was as follows. He breakfasted at seven o'clock in the morning, and after that spent the daylight hours supervising his draughtsmen. (Many of the drawings were made close to London, particularly of the Duke of Northumberland's trees at Syon and at Conrad Loddige's nursery at Hackney, though sometimes he travelled far afield.) At eight o'clock in the evening he returned home and dined. Then, after a brief rest, he set about his writing (much of it dictated to Jane) until two or three in the morning.

No fortune resulted, however; on the contrary, at its conclusion, Loudon was £10,000 in debt. His creditors pursued him; he was, however, able to fend them off by selling the work outright. But the long anticipated profit never materialised.

On and on went this dynamo, still full of energy in spite of steadily failing health—for bronchitis was now added to his other troubles. Sometimes he would be laying out estates, or public parks, or botanical gardens (such were the Derby Arboretum and, earlier on, the Birmingham Botanical Gardens). Another problem was that *The Gardener's Magazine*, having pioneered the way, was no longer successful, for more up-to-date rivals had caught the public taste. The books, articles and pamphlets still flowed forth. No one knows quite how many he wrote; they ranged with the same standard of excellency over gardening, farming and architecture.

By 1842 his health was so poor that he visited the south-western counties. Steadily his debts decreased; hope came of a more restful old age. And then one of his biggest creditors, who had been prepared to wait for his money, in turn went bankrupt. This man's representatives pressed Loudon for immediate payment—or else threatened bankruptcy and imprisonment.

His health was now failing rapidly; no longer could he travel. Yet he was able to stave off disaster by undertaking still more work; like so many pioneers in that most gentle of arts, gardening, he had courage greater than more warlike men.

At midnight on 13th December, 1843, as usual he stood by his desk dictating to Jane. He stumbled, and as he fell she caught his worn, shattered body. Within a moment he had died in her arms.

That is the story of Mr. and Mrs. Loudon. His own and their joint writings were something quite new in gardening; I do not think that they have since been exceeded in quantity and certainly their standard of clarity and accuracy has never been surpassed. It would be well if the many gardening journalists of today could follow them in this example.

We now come, rather sadly, to the days when the name of Mrs. Loudon became well-known as a writer on her own account. With Agnes, the daughter of the marriage, she stayed on at the house in Bayswater. Friends rallied round and helped her through the financial difficulties that followed her husband's death. She had already written a book called *Gardening for Ladies* and now followed this with more. In several of these, lithography, the new process which provided us with the first comparatively cheap method of colour printing, was used. In 1846 appeared her *British Wild Flowers*. This had many charming colour plates drawn by Noel Humphries, a talented artist who, like Jane, came from Birmingham. But the most delightful of her books is *The Ladies' Flower Garden*, in four large volumes—though what it has to do with women rather than with men gardeners I have never discovered. The work consists of many beautifully drawn colour plates showing groups of ornamental flowers. (The names of the artists seem to be unknown.) The text describes these flowers, their habits, histories and cultivation in a pleasant and well-informed manner. The titles of the volumes are *Greenhouse Plants*, *Bulbs*, *Annuals*, and *Perennials*. Her husband would have delighted in the accuracy and gay colour of the plates, and he would have approved the precision of the text. Reading it today makes us realise that though we have since gained a great many new plants, we have let a number of the early Victorians slip from our gardens.

Another delightful little book was *The Lady's Country Companion*. It was written in the form of letters to "dear Annie", who was a daughter of one of the newly rich town-dwellers. She married and went to live in a big country house. How she disliked it all after the town and what puzzles country life set her! The letters tell her just what to do—how big, gloomy pines near the house must be pulled down to let in light, how to cope with interfering neighbours and the crosspatch of an old gardener. And Annie was urged to occupy her spare time with country pastimes, keeping bees and goldfish, boating and skating. Above all, of course, she must make herself a lovely garden. It is in this garden, "now so brilliant with bright scarlet verbenas and golden yellow calceolarias, that you can scarcely gaze at it in the sunshine", where we finally take leave of a now contented Annie.

And as we read this book, we hear echoes of events and difficulties experienced long ago, when Birmingham-bred Jane Webb had to move out to the Worcestershire countryside and fend for her ailing father and her family.

These last cheerful and colourful books show no trace of what must have been a hard and difficult life. In spite of it, I think that she must have been a happy woman. She surely enjoyed the work that had occupied her life. She has, too, her little niche in fame, in addition to being one of the partners in "Mr. and Mrs. Loudon", in her own right as Mrs. Loudon whose books were on all Victorian bookshelves. She died, still at her home in Bayswater, on a July day in 1858.

JOSEPH PAXTON

The tale of Mr. and Mrs. Loudon is hardly what the world calls a "success story". Of material prosperity they only gained a modest share, though no one could seriously question the success of their work and writings.

Joseph Paxton, on the other hand, lived a life that might have come from an old-fashioned book of fairy-stories. Of humble origins, he became a knight and an intimate friend of the highest in the land. Born poor, almost all that he touched, if it did not turn to gold as in the story, at least brought him riches. Where Loudon by circumstances was forced to theorise and to write, Paxton was in a position to be a man of practice and affairs. Both had alike an immense influence on the gardens of Victoria's reign and even afterwards. At the time, and for long after, few would have doubted that Paxton was by far the more important. But the years have a way of turning things back to front: while Paxton's huge conservatories have tumbled down, Loudon's ideas and his huge book on trees remain important and alive; and the magazines and writings of Paxton, in spite of their lavish colour plates, have not, in the eyes of today, the charm and artistry of those produced by Mrs. Loudon. Yet Joseph Paxton still remains a great pioneer, a fine and generous character, a true hero of romance in real life.

He was born, in 1801, of humble farming stock, near the Duke of

Bedford's park at Woburn. He was the seventh son in a large family. His mother, it seems, had been a spirited girl, for she had run away to marry. His father died when he was still a boy, leaving those of the family still at home in poverty. Joseph was sent to an elder brother to be brought up. Here he worked on a farm—and was treated so harshly that he ran away. Of those hard times he spoke but little. Once, in prosperous years long afterwards, when dining in luxury, he unexpectedly turned to his daughter: "You never know how much nourishment there is in a turnip until you have had to live on it," he said.

Eventually, the runaway boy seems to have gone back to his family and then to work in the gardens of Battlesden Park in Bedfordshire. From there he moved to Woodhall, in Hertfordshire, where the head gardener seems to have been an exceptionally capable and friendly man, from whom the youth learned much.

A problem remains. In later years Paxton stands out as a well-educated man. He corresponded on equal terms with able botanists. He was concerned with several learned publications. How the beginnings of this education were picked up in those wandering early days remains a mystery.

Our next glimpse of him is back at Battlesden, now just twenty-one. He is no longer an underling, but supervising the construction of a lake. Then, a little after, we find him as a foreman at the Horticultural Society's new gardens at Chiswick—having, alas, added two years to his real age to get the job! There is no doubt, as we shall see, that he was a very capable foreman. All the same, the wages were low, with but little prospect of improvement. And on improvement Paxton had set his mind. By 1826 he had pretty well made up his mind that the United States of America held a better future for one of his disposition. But just at that moment, his fairy-godmother decided to take a hand in his life and turn the rest of it into a fairy-story.

Or, perhaps we should say, his fairy-godfather. The Horticultural Society leased the site of its gardens from the Duke of Devonshire. They lay next to his own house, where he often stayed when not at his country seat, Chatsworth. The young foreman worked in the Arboretum, taking particular care of the new trees, shrubs and climbers then beginning to arrive, thanks to the energies of Joseph Sabine. Into this part of the Society's gardens opened the gate which the Duke used when taking a stroll, which, though not particularly interested in gardening, he often did. The polite but never obsequious foreman, a stocky, good-looking young man, attracted his attention. He was knowledgeable and intelligent. He spoke well and sensibly. On this day in the spring of 1826 the Duke was rather worried. He had been chosen to represent his King and country at the crowning of Nicholas, Emperor of Russia. It was a rather ticklish assignment, for the relations between Britain and Russia were rather ruffled. The Government hoped that the wealthy and talented Duke, who was a friend of the new Emperor, would both represent Britain with due magnificence and smooth things over. At that very moment the post of head gardener at Chatsworth fell vacant; the Duke wished to fill it before he went. Making a sudden decision, he asked the young foreman whether he would care for the post.

Paxton was a man of courage and resource. The change from being an ill-paid foreman, only just twenty-three years old, to that of head gardener at Chatsworth, one of the most sumptuous houses and estates in England, must have presented itself to him as a transformation scene quite as alarming as it was magnificent.

The young man accepted. He took the coach for Derbyshire. The Duke sailed for Russia.

What sort of place was Chatsworth—with which the name of Joseph Paxton is today almost as closely associated as is that of its owners, the great family of Cavendish, Dukes of Devonshire?

A century and a quarter before Paxton rolled out of London, a certain Charles Leigh had described the place. He tells us that it is set in a valley among the hills of Derbyshire where they rise towards the Peak.

"Chatsworth," he wrote, "like a sun in an hazy air, adds lustre to those dusky mountains ..." The gardens, he continues, are "very delightful, pleasant and stately, adorned with exquisite water-works; the first we observe is Neptune with his sea-nymphs from whence, by the turning of a cock, immediately issue forth columns of water which seemed to fall upon sea-weeds. Not far from this is another pond, where sea-horses continually roll. Near to this stands a tree, composed of copper, which exactly resembles a willow; by the turning of a cock each leaf distils continually drops of water, and lively represents a shower of rain. . . . We come to a cascade, at the top of which stand two sea-nymphs, with each a jar under the arm; the water falling thence, whilst they seem to squeeze the vessels, produces a loud rumbling noise, like what we may imagine of the Egyptian or Indian cataracts . . . There is another pond, wherein is Mercury pointing at the Gods and throwing up water. Besides, there are several statues of gladiators, with the muscles of the body very lively displayed in their different postures . . ."

What a fairyland—and what a responsibility for young Joseph, when we remember, too, the more ordinary parts of the garden—the orangeries, vineries, lawns and the huge kitchen garden.

Paxton arrived at half-past four on a May morning. No one was about, so he climbed into the garden over the greenhouse gate. He explored his new care, and looked around the outside of the great mansion, described by Leigh, begun by the first Duke of Devonshire in 1687 and to which additions were even now still being made. Then he sought out the kitchen garden, some way from the house, climbed over its wall, and when the gardeners came at six o'clock, set them to work. Next, back in the pleasure gardens, he had the foreman in charge of the waterworks "turn the cocks" and "play them" for him. Finally, he visited the housekeeper, old Mrs. Gregory, and she provided breakfast. Her niece, Sarah Bown, was with her. Joseph at once fell in love with her, and she with him; it was by now just nine o'clock.

In less than a year the new head gardener (engaged at 25s. a week, with a cottage) married Miss Sarah Bown, quiet, distinguished, older than he was—and with a nice little fortune of her own. At first, of course, no one approved. Something much better than an unknown gardener was expected for her. But Sarah proved a remarkable wife to him. She had, for one thing, an intimate knowledge of Chatsworth and its contents and affairs. The famous contents of the house had bred in her a love of works of art and good taste. Her inborn knowledge of all its affairs, with her business abilities, proved invaluable. They did, indeed, live superbly happily ever after, and Sarah's acumen and sense always lay behind the creative genius and imagination of her husband.

The Duke, as we have said, was not interested in gardening. The gardens at Chatsworth showed it. A large body of gardeners had spent an easy time for the last few years doing the minimum of work. The place was neglected. The new head gardener set vigorously about improving the situation. He was a fair and straight-dealing young man, who throughout his life considered the interests of those who worked for him. Under him the staff now set to work with a will to bring back to Chatsworth gardens their former glory. It was uphill work. All was far from well behind the grand façade. Four pineapple houses were found to be in bad condition. Two big vineries carried only eight bunches of grapes. Work seemed to have stopped still at the turn of the century, and none of the new plants now arriving from overseas were to be found in the collections—eight rhododendrons only, and not a single camellia!

In the meantime, the Duke was having a gloriously successful time in Russia. The entertaining by his mission was on such a scale that it outdid all that of the other countries. He spent, and did not grudge it, £50,000 of his own money in addition to the official expenses granted by the Government. Thanks to his high spirits and energy, his errand to Nicholas was a triumph. In December he was back at Chatsworth. "My new gardener", he wrote in his diary, "has made a great change."

Paxton's employer was William Spencer, sixth Duke of Devonshire, the "bachelor duke". For in spite of his talents, charms and great fortune, he never married. Son of that Georgiana, Duchess of Devonshire, painted by Sir Joshua Reynolds and Gainsborough, he inherited her gay and extravagant nature. From his father, of the line of Cavendishes (who had from time to time risked much in standing for the rights of the common people), he inherited a usually concealed serious and religious side to his nature. Melancholy often lay not far behind the gaiety—while deafness also helped to make him a man always a little apart from his fellows.

The Duke soon realised that his choice of Paxton was right. He became an important and trusted servant. The greenhouses were soon sound again. The kitchen garden, long subject to floods when the river rose (there was talk of moving it to another site), was now by Paxton's ingenuity kept dry without the expense of a move; new and rare plants were added to the collection. The woods had been neglected; Paxton took them in hand and paid for some of the numerous additions and alterations with the timber that was sold. He moved big trees to new situations (the local wiseacres knew that they would die—you can see them flourishing today!).

As the years went on, Paxton was more and more consulted by the Duke, who would send for him to come to London. When difficulties arose in the work on the estate, Paxton always seemed to be able to find a way out. The Duke became more and more interested in gardening. By 1834 he was himself buying seeds and plants in Paris, and sent for Paxton—urgently in need of his advice. The gardener had never yet travelled abroad—but he was soon to find himself at ease and in good company in Paris as at Chatsworth. Before long gardening became the Duke's ruling passion; his ingenious, reliable and charming gardener his closest companion. Together they travelled to see other gardens—sometimes in England, later on the Continent.

In the meantime, Paxton had entered the journalistic world, through his friendship with William Bradbury, the founder of *Punch*. Perhaps because of the success of Paxton's new periodical, *The Horticultural Register*, J.C. Loudon published a very harsh criticism of Paxton and Chatsworth in his own *The Gardener's Magazine*. A wordy battle followed; the great Loudon, we must admit, was put in his place by his junior. However, neither man was of the kind to harbour a grievance, and before long they were happy friends, Paxton often writing notes for *The Gardener's Magazine* on interesting plants with which he succeeded at Chatsworth, and Loudon paying tributes to the glories and greenhouses of Chatsworth. When, not long afterwards, Loudon died, it was Paxton who took the initiative in helping his widow.

We have mentioned the greenhouses of Chatsworth. The Duke's enthusiasm for them, once his head gardener had initiated him into their marvels, was to play an important part in Paxton's later life. The early lack of them at Chatsworth was soon remedied by new structures built by Paxton from his own ingenious designs.

The Duke, like others of the nobility, and other rich men were now vying with one another in the magnificence of their collections of plants to fill their new greenhouses. Paxton and the Duke, ambitious as ever to go one better, decided to send out their own collector to India. An intelligent young Chatsworth gardener, John Gibson, was chosen. The Duke's influence, of course, opened all doors for him; he travelled to India with the new Governor-General and his suite. At that time the head of the Calcutta Botanical Garden was the eminent Dr. Wallich, who not only maintained a rich and rare collection of plants in the gardens, but had a wide knowledge of the localities where new treasures, particularly orchids, might be found. For his part, Gibson took with him as a present to Dr. Wallich a rich collection of seeds and plants from Chatsworth that would be likely to succeed at Calcutta.

Just at the moment when Gibson arrived, one of Wallich's greatest treasures, a tree, *Amherstia nobilis*, was flowering in the gardens for the first time. The doctor had found this, some years before, while he had been on an expedition to Burma to study the valuable teak forests. Covered with geranium-red flowers, it was growing in a monastery garden. The blossoms were being offered before the images of Buddha. Paxton and the Duke were covetous on hearing of this new wonder.

Gibson was away for two years. He then came back with a grand collection of plants, mostly orchids—and two Amherstias, particularly carefully packed and labelled, one for the Duke and the other for the East India Company. All at Chatsworth were excited by the news. On his arrival, Gibson reported a tragedy. One Amherstia was dead—the one destined for Chatsworth. The Duke at once wrote to the Directors of the East India Company. There was, he said, now only one living plant in England, which was theirs, and whatever happened, it must be kept alive; who, he argued, could nurture it better than Gibson, the man who had brought it home, under his care in the greenhouse at Chatsworth? Paxton took coach to London so that he might be on the spot at this critical moment. Happily, the directors of the Company yielded their treasure to the Duke. Paxton arrived early in the morning to find the Amherstia installed in the Painted Hall at Devonshire House, with the Duke breakfasting beside it. All that day the great ones of the gardening world came to pay court to the wonder from Burma. Then Paxton himself safely conveyed the tree and the big case in which it grew to Chatsworth. There the plant thrived—but, alas, never flowered. Twelve years later Chatsworth lost this honour to a much smaller plant grown by Mrs. Lawrence in her famous garden at Ealing Park!

Plant-hunting was now in the air. The Duke and Paxton next interested themselves in an expedition to the Pacific Coast of North America. The sad death of Douglas had cut short his work there. He had collected but small quantities of seed from many of the trees and plants that he had found. They consequently remained rare and extremely expensive. Paxton considered that if two men working as a pair went and followed in his footsteps, the difficulties experienced by a lone hand would then be eased and a rich harvest result. An expedition was financed by the Duke and a group of land-owners, together with nurserymen, who would share the collections. Ample funds were thus available. Paxton, in whose mind the undertaking originated, supervised the planning. Peter Banks and Robert Wallace, two more of the clever young gardeners that he was now gathering round him at Chatsworth, were chosen. The pair duly wrote home of their safe arrival in Canada. Then came silence—to be broken by the tragic news that both had been drowned when their boat had been smashed on a rock in the Columbia River.

In the story of Kew Gardens we have told of the deliberation and activities that eventually placed Sir William Hooker as their Director. Paxton took a part in these, for he was a member of the Commission that made an inquiry into their use and management. His abilities clearly impressed certain high authorities dealing with the matter, for he was offered the post of Royal Gardener at Windsor Castle. Here was a difficult decision to be taken. Still a comparatively young man, he saw before him the highest position to which a gardener could aspire. He was ambitious. Should he leave the Duke, who had done so much for him? He hesitated, but not for long. Chatsworth had made him what he was, and at Chatsworth he would stay while he was wanted.

In 1836 work began on a new great conservatory. It was to be 277 feet long and 123 feet wide. The ridge of the glass roof was 67 feet above the ground at its highest point. A coach and horse could drive through it from a gallery, whose stairway was concealed within rockwork, visitors could stand marvelling at the exotic display below. The building took several years to complete. While Paxton was still engaged on it, the Duke set out on a long European tour. Quite unexpectedly, Paxton received a summons from Geneva to go and join his master. Sarah was upset, and to Paxton the time was inopportune. Yet, with both husband and wife, their loved Duke's word was law. Paxton set out—not to return to his Sarah until many weeks had passed. Switzerland, the Alps, Italy, Malta and Turkey were explored. The once garden boy now moved easily and unaffectedly among the aristocracy of the ancient civilisations of the West. Long letters home to Sarah told of their adventures. By now, he had become the Duke's most intimate friend and adviser.

In 1843 the Queen and Prince Albert paid a visit to Chatsworth. The month appointed was December—hardly the time of year to visit a place particularly famed for its gardens! But, sparing no expense, the Duke and Paxton decided to do their best. The Queen and her party were met at the station by a coach and six, with eight outriders. Guns—arranged for by Paxton—thundered out a royal salute as they entered the park. After dinner, Victoria was led to the window. All was dark. Then, in a moment, the falls, cascades, fountains and statues burst gloriously into light. Gold, crimson, green and blue flames were reflected in the water. Then the party walked into the new conservatory, where thousands of lamps flickering among the exotic plants brought a tropical scene to England's midwinter. The display was stupendous and long remembered.

The following morning the Duke of Wellington, who had come with the Queen, walked round the gardens. To his amazement all was normal again by daylight—no trace of all the litter and paraphernalia of the previous day remained; everything was tidy. "I should have liked your gardener as one of my generals," said the soldier duke to the bachelor duke.

From now on a Paxton other than the gardener appeared—one whose career we shall not follow. It is that of the railway pioneer, industrialist and man of national affairs. Yet, all the time, Paxton remained a gardener, and the Duke's gardener, at heart.

Nothing illustrates this more clearly than the story of the famous giant water-lily, *Victoria amazonica* (or *regia*, as it was once called, after the Queen). This plant, with its enormous leaves, was discovered on the River Amazon in the early eighteen-thirties. It was one of those plants which, like Amherstia, had excited the gardening world. The first attempts to grow it here failed. At last the skilful Sir William Hooker raised seedlings at Kew. One was offered to the Duke of Devonshire.

Paxton himself—by now a man of consequence—travelled to Kew and collected the seedling; at Chatsworth he himself planted it. The seedling soon outgrew the first tank that had been specially built for it. On 2nd November, 1849, Paxton triumphed. *Victoria* flowered for him. The failure with Amherstia was offset. He wrote to the Duke, who was in Ireland, "No words can describe the grandeur and beauty of the plant." He fetched Sir William Hooker from Kew—"The sight is worth a journey of a thousand miles." The Queen graciously permitted Mr. Paxton to take a flower and a leaf for her to see. The giant leaves, up to six feet across, were as outstanding as the flower; on 22nd November the Duke, who had speeded home to see it, stood Miss Paxton, then seven years old, upon one. Yet so fragile was its surface that she had to stand on a metal lid so that the fabric should not be damaged, the water let through and the leaf sink.

Paxton's success in winning the race to flower *Victoria* had an important consequence. The lily grew so big that the Duke decided to build a new conservatory specially to house it. This was a most ingenious building, entirely of iron and glass. Paxton, as we have seen, had built and experimented with several greenhouses and conservatories. This one, embodying all his experience, was something quite new. The novel system of construction, as Paxton was fond of explaining, was inspired by the natural structure of the ribs in the leaves of the giant lily itself. His acute powers of observation were soon to have unexpected consequences far beyond the building of a greenhouse. For at that time England was excited by the talk of a huge exhibition. The bold imagination of Prince Albert was largely responsible for the idea. It was to show the world, and our own people, the wonderful state of our arts, sciences and manufactures. It was to be called the Great Exhibition and was to be held in a building in Hyde Park. The idea was so startling, the Prince such a remarkable (and therefore not very popular) man, that a great section of influential opinion was opposed to it. Paxton, who was of the same school of thought as the Prince Consort, supported the project enthusiastically. The greatest problem that had to be faced was the provision of a building large enough to house it. There was much argument, but at last the type of building was decided upon. Yet it was generally held by those in a position to know to be unsound, extravagantly expensive and unsuitable. The hostile criticism of the enemies of the plan that it aroused was indeed justified. The prospects for the Prince's exhibition looked bad. Paxton was among those who said unhesitatingly that a mistake was being made. Through the influence of a few men who knew his worth, he was able to put his own ideas before the committee. "If you give me a chance," he said, "I will bring you my own plans complete in nine days hence." The committee scarcely took him seriously—but gave him the opportunity he asked.

A day or two later, Paxton was attending a meeting of a railway company in Derby. He was seen to be busy scribbling away on a nice white sheet of blotting paper. His colleagues thought he was taking notes of what was passing; asking, therefore, for his opinion on the matter under discussion, which he seemed to be following so closely, they were amazed when he held up the sheet. "This," he said, "is a design for the Great Industrial Exhibition to be held in Hyde Park." This famous sheet of blotting paper has been preserved; it shows the conservatory built to house the giant water-lily magnified many times until it was big enough to cover the exhibition.

The story of the battle to get this plan accepted and of how the marvellous Crystal Palace at last rose in but seventeen weeks is not the story of Paxton, head gardener at Chatsworth, but of his rise to become Sir Joseph Paxton, eminent Victorian man of the world, Member of Parliament for Coventry, and director of companies, living in great style at a fine house in Sydenham, of whom you may find something in ordinary history books.

Successful—yes. But happy? In 1858 the Duke died. Paxton, his efficient servant to the last, organised the grandiose funeral faultlessly down to its smallest detail. There was now another Duke reigning at Chatsworth; Paxton resigned his position there. No bachelor Duke, no Chatsworth; other successes could never make up for those losses.

Then Paxton himself, not yet an old man, began to fail in health. One May day in 1865 he made his last public appearance. It was in a wheeled chair, at a flower-show, to gaze once more on the things that had brought him happiness above all. It was on a day in May, too, that as a young man he had climbed over a garden wall.

In the following June he died. He was taken back to Chatsworth. In the churchyard, next to William Spencer, sixth Duke of Devonshire, they laid his gardener, Sir Joseph Paxton. The new Duke followed him to his grave, accompanied by many great men who had been his friends. The fairy-tale about a garden-boy had ended.

Paxton was a pioneer because, for one thing, along with Loudon, he was the leading force in applying the developments of science and mechanics to gardening.

Never in history had such perfect greenhouses been built and the plants—fruits, flowers and vegetables alike—so scientifically and skilfully cultivated. The example set by Chatsworth was followed all over the land. Paxton, too, was a pioneer in acquiring and planting those new introductions from abroad which have altered the face of Britain. So much for Paxton's influence on the gardens of the wealthy—the remains of the old rich aristocracy and the new rich manufacturers and business men. Through the publications and periodicals with which he was associated, however, his ideas were given to a much wider circle; even today many of them will be found embodied in and inspiring the policy of *The Gardener's Chronicle*, happily still vigorous as when Paxton and his friend Lindley brought out the first issue in 1841.

CHAPTER 11

To China Again

MISSIONARIES, CONSULS AND CUSTOMS OFFICERS

The average garden today, particularly if many shrubs are cultivated, will probably contain more different kinds of plants which originate, at least in part, from China than from Europe. Our present-day roses, chrysanthemums and rhododendrons are but three examples.

We have already learned how Robert Fortune brought a number of new flowers from China, but he travelled only by the coast, the eastern part of China. Pekin in the north, where Father d'Incarville and a few others penetrated, is also not far inland. The early collectors reaped a wonderful harvest. Travel into the interior was not then allowed, and the lands of western China remained unvisited. Even scientists scarcely suspected what lay there; yet, as one traveller who visited the region later was to write, Aladdin's cave contained nothing equal to the glut of flowering treasures that grew there; even "a pale imitation of the scene in England, and men would scarcely believe their eyes."

The pioneers who sought it out were mostly officials and missionaries by profession, and enthusiastic amateur botanists in their spare time. Later the scientific and systematic plant-collectors followed them up and brought home their spoils. But while gardeners know the names of at least a few of the collectors—Wilson, Forrest, Farrer, Kingdon-Ward and Rock, for example—we may mention first some of those less known amateurs who were the first to go.

One was an official in the English consular service, Henry Fletcher Hance. More important than his own collection of specimens was, however, the fact that he made a not unpleasant nuisance of himself by asking everyone whom he thought might be the slightest use to collect and bring him specimens when they travelled. By this means he formed a big herbarium, each specimen labelled with the full details of how and where it was growing. By this means botanists were first able to form a picture of the plant life in the large unexplored districts of western China. In turn, this picture painted by botanists was later to cause gardeners to despatch collectors so that they might have, if not the whole canvas, at least some of the colours that went to its painting.

Hance must have been an odd man. After an education in London and on the Continent, he went to China in 1844 at the early age of seventeen. There he lived and worked with only occasional visits to England until his death. Word-perfect in Latin, Greek, French and German—though he lived forty-three years in China, he always refused to learn Chinese. From the number of people who collected and brought him plants, he must have had a persuasive manner.

He lived in the district of Canton, near the mouth of one of the several giant rivers that wind their long ways from south China and the neighbouring states up into western China and the borders of Tibet. It was on the plants of those areas, therefore, that Hance became an authority.

There was, of course, the other way to the heart of China, the Russian approach from Siberia. Many important journeys of Chinese exploration were made by Russian explorers. In St. Petersburg was a man whose activities were similar to those of Hance, Carl Johan Maximowicz, though indeed Maximowicz did make some important collecting trips himself. He was born in 1827—the same year as Hance—and was a professional botanist. The two men never met, but corresponded continuously.

It was, therefore, the activities of these two, with their steadily mounting collections of dried, flattened specimens, which brought to the West a realisation that the earlier collectors had picked but a handful of China's flowers.

Maximowicz, Hance and their friends for long worked under impossibly restrictive conditions. Most of China was in a wild, lawless state at the mercy of petty chieftains. The inefficient central government, instead of carrying out the terms of its treaties with the European trading states, was awkward and obstructive. At last Britain and France sent an army. The Chinese forces collapsed, and in 1860 a new treaty was made. Maximowicz and Hance must have been overjoyed at the terms. Foreigners were now to be allowed much greater freedom of movement in the interior. The European consular services were strengthened. Religious missions were permitted to increase their work and members, while an organisation, the Imperial Maritime Customs, was set up under an Englishman, Sir Robert Hart. All this meant that more men would come into China who could be pressed into service as collectors—apart from others who might collect and botanise independently.

Five of them are so interwoven with the history of Chinese plants, many of which are now almost commonplace in our gardens, that some space must be given to them. Four were French Jesuit missionaries, the other a British official. Between them they form the links between the work of Hance and the two great collectors whom we shall discuss shortly.

Father Jean Pierre Armand David came from the Basses-Pyrénées. He was an accomplished organist, a zealous missionary, and one of the finest all-round naturalists who ever worked in China. Visitors to Whipsnade will know of Father David's deer—but we must pass over that interesting discovery and, indeed, his early Chinese journeys made soon after his arrival there in the same year that the treaty was signed. Important though the results were for geographers, geologists and zoologists, his later travels were of greater interest botanically.

His importance for gardeners lies in a journey that he made in 1868 to the remote alps which lie bordering China and eastern Tibet. No scientist had ever been there before; we are fortunate, indeed, that the first was to be a man of David's capabilities. It was a visit that opened men's eyes to the fabulous riches of the district. David spent six months at a place called Mupin, and used his spare time there in systematically examining one comparatively small mountain area. He found and collected an immense number of new plants. One of the most remarkable was a tree, named after him *Davidia*—a discovery that was later to bring about the search for its seeds which opened the great career of E. H. Wilson, of whom more will be said below. Many hitherto unknown rhododendrons, lillies and poppies also figure in his collections.

This great naturalist was a frail and often sick man. Ill-health forced him to leave China for France after spending only fourteen years there. He was quiet and unassuming, absurdly shy of parading his voluminous knowledge. Instead of telling people what he had learned from his own travels and discoveries, he was modestly content to be their questioner. A bit queer, his fellow-missionaries thought him—always quietly seeking animals, plants, rocks.

Under the most difficult conditions, Father David collected his information which laid the broad foundations of our knowledge of the fauna and flora of China. He himself collected, preserved and despatched to France some three thousand different kinds of plants—of which a third never arrived, having been lost by one or other of the many hazards of the journey. David did not himself introduce many living plants, but his discoveries and the records that he made of their localities were of great service to later collectors.

Father Jean Marie Delavay, like David, also came from a mountainous home—Haute-Savoie. Unlike David, he was essentially a botanist, collecting and studying extensively when not busy with his duties. In 1867 he was stationed not far from Hance, who at once pressed him into his services and gave him encouragement. Unhappily, Delavay shortly after met David, and was persuaded to send his collections not to Hance but to Paris. This was a tragedy, for Hance dealt with all the material that he received methodically and carefully. In Paris the opposite was the case. Delavay's boxes of specimens still lay unopened years after they had been received while many of the seeds that he sent home were effectively killed by ignorant gardeners in the Jardin des Plantes.

This sad mismanagement was a poor reward for Delavay's patience and industry, as well as an obstruction to the study of Chinese botany, for he sent home no fewer than 200,000 specimens of plants. Each

Buddleia davidii, named in honour of Father Armand David and introduced by Father Jean Soulié

one he picked, pressed and mounted himself with exquisite care and skill; when at last they were examined, the perfection of his work had happily resulted in their condition remaining unharmed. His notes on the plants, too, were supremely clear and well written.

Delavay's most important work was completed while he was stationed at a mission in Yunnan for ten years. He was therefore able to gain knowledge of the plants in his district throughout the seasons, year after year. As an instance of his thoroughness, he climbed a particular mountain near his home and collected the plants on it at every season of the year and from every angle. In all he made the ascent sixty times, enabling him to give an intimate description of its flora.

In 1886 Delavay caught bubonic plague and never properly recovered his health. A few years after he returned to France, and there lost the use of his right arm. This, for a man so skilled with his hands, must have been a dreadful fate. Undaunted, he returned to China, and continued to collect plants almost until the day of his death.

Father Delavay was little known and had but few friends, for the reason that practically all his life was spent in wild places remote from fellow-Europeans. Carrying his religion to and working among a strange people, and studying the plants which surrounded them, provided his solitary life with more satisfaction than Western civilisation could give.

Father Delavay's many discoveries include two plants that have since become immensely popular, *Primula malacoides* (later introduced into England by George Forrest) and the blue poppy, *Meconopsis betonicifolia*. His name is honoured in many other plants—*Paeonia delavayi, Osmanthus delavayi* and *Incarvillea delavayi* are but three that we are likely to meet in gardens.

A contrast in many ways was Paul Guillaume Farges. Out of a lifetime spent in China he spent only eleven years in collecting plants. Though arriving in 1867, it was not until 1892, when he was stationed in the province of Szechuan, that he started collecting. The district was stricken by poverty and famine. A capable and energetic man, he was soon successful in organising relief in the district. The surrounding country happened to be very rich in trees and shrubs: Farges collected these and other plants assiduously. By 1903 he had collected some four thousand species. Then, after he had been appointed almoner at Chungking hospital, for some reason he entirely ceased collecting. In the short period during which he worked, however, he was fortunate in coming upon a particularly high proportion of trees and shrubs—rhododendrons in particular—that have since grown successfully and proved popular in our gardens. *Decaisnea fargesii,* with long, blue pods, is a handsome shrub that commemorates this botanist.

The fourth missionary-botanist was still another type of man. Father Jean Andre Soulié spent an adventurous life on the borders of Tibet and China. His work was principally as a medical missionary, but he was at the same time a keen botanist and able collector. More of a man of the world than the others, his fortune was to be popular and welcome in whatever circles he moved. Whether among his colleagues, the Buddhist monks, or the common people, he was always cheerfully at home. His success among the natives was helped by his fame as a healer. Travelling widely up and down the dangerous borderland in the course of his duties, wherever he went plant-collecting occupied his spare time. Soulié made other than these official journeys. His build and the cast of his features, helped by high cheek-bones, was somewhat Oriental. Aided by this appearance and a mastery of local dialects, he several times travelled successfully disguised as a native. Thus he traversed almost secret passes and routes on the forbidden margins of Tibet. His daring was great; one false step disclosing that he was a European and his life would have been forfeit.

In ten years Soulié collected seven thousand specimens. He also sent home seeds of plants, but the remote districts in which he worked made it impossible for him to forward many. Quite the most famous plant that he introduced was the honey-scented purple buddleia, now so much at home in our gardens that it seeds itself freely. The botanical name of this, *Buddleia davidii,* appropriately honours Soulié's fellow-countryman.

His fate was tragic. In 1905 there was trouble and fighting between Tibet and China. Tibetan monks crossed the frontier. Soulié was warned and could have escaped. But he delayed his flight to pack his collections; the Tibetans arrived too soon and Soulié was caught. After suffering days of torture, he was shot.

The last, and the most important, of these spare-time botanists and collectors was an Irishman, Augustine Henry, from Londonderry.

After a brilliant career at Belfast University he turned to medicine
and qualified as a doctor. He found that he disliked medical practice,
however, and gave it up. He seems to have been rather at a loose end
when by chance he heard of a vacancy in the new Chinese Customs
Service under Sir Robert Hart. "A well-educated man, with some
knowledge of medicine" was wanted. Henry applied and was given
the post.

He was sent to Ichang, high up the Yangtse River, as Customs and
Medical Officer. His duties finished quite early in the afternoon, and,
it seems, he got bored. Roaming about in the evenings, he began to
take notice of the remarkable vegetation of the district. He collected
sprays of those plants that attracted him, took them home and tried to
get them named. All he could learn was their Chinese local names. So,
after collecting together a good number of specimens, modestly and,
as he considered, greatly daring, he sent a box of them to the Royal
Botanic Gardens at Kew with a request that they might be correctly
named. Fortunately the authorities there were very different from those
in Paris. They were at once interested in the plants that this botanical
novice sent them. They replied with the names as far as they were
able to give them, offered him advice and help on how to go about
his work, and urged him to send more specimens along. So, almost
by accident, Henry was started on the path towards becoming one of
the greatest authorities on the plants of western China.

While he lived at Ichang he searched the famed gorges where the
Yangtse River breaks through into the plain. In addition to collecting
the wealth of plants growing there his men were carefully trained to
be on the look-out for anything unusual and, when spotted, to pick it
in the proper manner so that a specimen might be carefully preserved
and sent to Kew. A pony boy proved particularly clever and helpful
to him in this work, but others were not equally so. One episode in
particular eventually caused a great deal of laughter. A native collector
brought Henry a flowering spray of a plant that seemed to be quite new.
The flower looked like a guelder rose, the leaf like a horse-chestnut.
Carefully pressed, the specimen eventually arrived at Kew. Here, said
the experts, is something absolutely new. Excitement was high, and
the name *Actinotinus sinensis* was coined specially for the novelty.
Then someone discovered that the new plant was, in fact, a guelder

rose flower joined with all the perfection of Chinese craftsmanship to a horse-chestnut leaf!

Henry was a man of enthusiasm, patience and great industry. He learned to speak the native language fluently and was given the Chinese rank of mandarin. His success in his official work led to promotion, which enabled him to travel widely. For a time he lived near an ancient and primitive tribe known as Lolos. He was able to mix with them, and compiled a dictionary of their language. He was also interested in zoology, and discovered a new kind of antelope. When, in 1900, this remarkable man retired from the Chinese Customs Service, he began a new and equally brilliant career as a pioneer of scientific forestry in the British Isles. But that is another story and we must return to his work on Chinese plants.

In all, he sent 158,000 dried and labelled specimens to the botanists at Kew. Literally hundreds of them were entirely new to science. Most important of all, English nurserymen and gardeners saw the results of his sendings and realised that many of the plants, which they saw to be of rare beauty, might be expected to grow in the British Isles. The missionaries and Henry had sent home seeds of no more than a handful of these treasures which showed promise. But these men were busily otherwise occupied, and were only part-time botanists. The time had now come to pick successors to Fortune and his like, and to send them up from the mouths of the great rivers on the coast, familiar to the older generation, high into the mountains of their headwaters. There, in western China, even in unapproachable Tibet, great prizes were to be sought. To achieve them would need courage and skilful planning. Adventurous men were needed, with a knowledge of botany and gardening.

They were, of course, forthcoming. Wilson, Forrest, Purdom, Farrer, Kingdon-Ward are among the great British names; while from the United States came men like Rock and Meyer.

In this book we are concerned only with pioneers, so E. H. Wilson and George Forrest, the two men first on the scene, must stand here as representatives of the pioneering of modern plant-collection.

E. H. WILSON

There is one kind of pioneer, quite important, about which we know very little—the nurserymen. We have, however, some records of the old firm of Veitch.

John Veitch came from Jedburgh in Scotland. At the end of the eighteenth century he was laying out gardens in the west country and soon afterwards founded a nursery—first near Broadclyst in Devon, where he had helped to lay out the now famous gardens at Killerton, and then at Exeter.

Successive generations of the family followed an enterprising policy. They were among the first to grasp that there was a great future for hardy foreign plants in British gardens. As early as 1840 they had sent a Cornishman, William Lobb, to South America so that he might obtain large quantities of seed of the monkey-puzzle tree. This had only just been introduced, and had become all the rage—young plants fetched high prices. Lobb was successful. Later he followed in Douglas's footsteps over North America, making large collections of the most popular of Douglas's introductions. One member of the family, John Gould Veitch, it was mentioned above, visited Japan in 1860, bringing back the golden-rayed lily, some ornamental maples, irises and flowering cherries. Charles Maries had been sent to China and Japan in 1877. In China, though he collected several important plants, he somehow entirely missed the treasures being unearthed by the French missionaries; he went right to the Ichang gorges of the Yangtse, stopped and reported to his employers on his return that there was little else new now left in China.

Sir John Henry Veitch, the head of the firm at the end of the last century, was one of those who were greatly impressed by the specimens sent to Kew by Augustine Henry. Above all David's tree took his fancy. The Davidia is also called the dove tree, the ghost tree and even the pocket-handkerchief tree. The name is due to the big white appendages that surround the small flower, making it a most lovely sight in spring.

Following the pioneering tradition of his firm, on 27th March, 1899, Sir Harry (as he was called) signed a contract with a young man, who had never been out of England, to proceed to China and collect seeds of Davidia.

The other signature on the document, that of Ernest Henry Wilson, marked the opening of the career of the first modern plant-collector.

Many of those who went overseas to collect plants spent their childhood among mountains, in Scotland and the high parts of France. They were therefore at home among the mountains of China or America.

Wilson was an exception, for he was born among the gentle midland Cotswolds, at Chipping Camden. He was apprenticed to a firm of nurserymen at Solihull in Warwickshire and moved on to the Botanical Gardens which then existed in Birmingham; while there he studied botany in the technical school. Transferring to Kew Gardens, he finally decided on a career as botany teacher. Just at that moment the firm of Veitch were inquiring for someone suitable as a collector. The Director of Kew recommended Wilson. So, after six months at the Veitch nursery at Coombe Wood in Devon, the contract to seek Davidia was signed.

Later in his life Wilson wrote an account of this journey. The story is so typical of the tales told by other modern plant-hunters that we may like to follow it.

Sir Harry Veitch's instructions were definite: to collect seeds of Davidia and not waste time on anything else. Sir Harry was no doubt influenced in his decision to get this plant by a statement made by the Keeper of the Kew Herbarium, who had examined the first specimens sent home by Henry; the tree was, he said, almost worthy of a special mission to China with a view to its introduction to European gardens.

Wilson's further instruction was to call on Dr. Henry at Szemao, in Yunnan, not far from the borders of Burma, and the other side of China from that known to Fortune.

Wilson sailed first to Boston, so that he might meet Dr. Charles Sargent, head of the Arnold Arboretum, where he had charge of one of the world's greatest collections of woody plants. Sargent was then probably the greatest living authority on trees and shrubs. He had himself travelled and collected in different parts of the world. Wilson spent five days with him, learning the "tricks of the trade", and beginning a lasting friendship with his American elder. Then he travelled across the American continent and on to Hongkong.

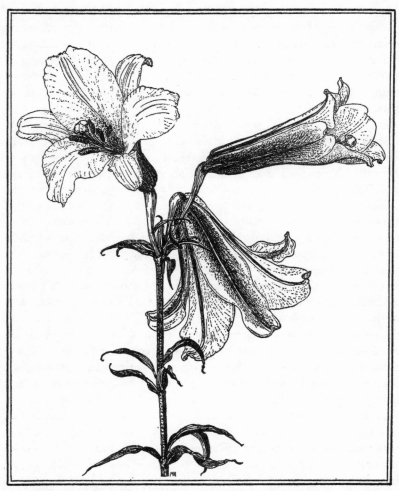

Lilium regale, E. H. Wilson's most famous introduction from China

"The holiday part of my journey is now over," he wrote, and indeed it was. He was to reach Dr. Henry by travelling up through Tonking in French Indo-China to the Chinese border, then across the province of Yunnan to Szemao. He was to sail up the Red River in one of the regular steamers as far as they plied, and then transfer to a native boat. The final stage to Szemao was to be overland on mule-back or sedan chair.

Hanoi, the capital of Tonking, was safely reached. Wilson was handicapped because he could not speak French, the language of the officials, nor, of course, any native dialect. But he heard the first rumours of trouble ahead. A railway from Hanoi up to the Chinese border was being surveyed. The Chinese did not like this threatened intrusion into their traditional privacy and were in an ugly mood. When the steamer with Wilson aboard reached a small French military post at Laokai, the news became worse. Foreigners had been attacked and a French customs house and consulate burned down. The French authorities, as a measure of safety, forbade all further travel.

The days of unactivity that followed were later described by Wilson as the worst period he suffered during his whole eleven years of plant-hunting. He was an inexperienced traveller embarking on a new and speculative enterprise. There was no Entente Cordiale with France in those days, and the officials suspected him of being an English spy. They repeatedly harried him—and the fact that he could not speak their language made matters no easier.

Laokai stands in low-lying, swampy country. The heat was extreme. No day passed without a tropical storm; scarcely a morning without the bugles sounding for the funeral of a fever-stricken soldier. The small steamer that left for Hanoi each Sunday was filled with sick. As the days dragged on, Wilson at last made his plans to join it and return home. He was actually writing letters to Veitch and Henry saying that his mission must be abandoned when, to his surprise, the French commandant granted him leave to proceed upstream.

Wilson, cheered and anxious to be off, now faced another setback. For fear of trouble and reprisals, no Chinese servant was willing to travel up-country with the European. So another month was wasted in fever-haunted Laokai. At last a Chinese came forward and offered his services. For some reason of his own, he was anxious to make the journey. He spoke little English, was clearly an opium addict, and the nearest thing to a reference that he was able to show was a document discharging him from the telegraph service for incompetency!

With him, however, Wilson set off. Rumours of murder and war abounded—fortunately, says Wilson, as he then knew nothing of the Chinese language he remained largely in blissful ignorance of many of the unpleasant happenings that were discussed. Untoward incidents were numerous: the native boat on which he travelled struck a rock in some rapids and nearly sank—but at last he arrived at Szemao, and met Henry. He learned a great deal from that experienced man—about Chinese ways as well as plants—and, of course, the situation of the one and only Davidia tree that Henry had ever seen, at the time when he was stationed at Ichang by the Yangtse gorges.

Wilson was now gaining experience of Chinese travel for himself by the hard way and, further fortified by the wisdom imparted to him by Henry, he made an easier and uneventful journey back to Hongkong. Here he prepared for the final assault on Davidia. (Incidentally, Wilson disobeyed Sir Harry Veitch's instructions and from Hongkong despatched a most interesting selection of plants collected on his trip to Henry. This was the first consignment of many, and demonstrated that, like Fortune, he had a remarkable skill in picking those subjects which were "good garden plants".)

In February 1900 Wilson arrived at Ichang for a two years' stay. He had with him a map, drawn by Henry on the page of a notebook. It covered an area as big as New York State. The country shown was one of wild, high mountains. Among them was marked the site of a solitary tree—the one and only Davidia. Wilson's objective, indeed, must have seemed like the needle in the haystack.

Wilson set sail from Ichang up the Yangtse on an April day on the first stage of his search. Twice his boat was badly damaged by rocks among the rapids and disaster was only just avoided. When the homeland of Davidia was reached, he found that the natives there were ready to make trouble at the slightest provocation; rioting had occurred in the district and a Christian missionary had been burned to death. But Wilson was now showing that understanding of the Chinese character which henceforth enabled him to move about among them so freely.

At last the very house was reached where Henry had been stopping twelve years before on the day when he had seen Davidia.

Did the inhabitants know it? Yes, they replied, we will take you to it.

As the party approached the spot, Wilson noticed a newly built house. By it was a stump. It was all that was left of the solitary Davidia. The trunk, he was told, had come in very handy for building the new house!

"I did not sleep that night," wrote Wilson.

He returned to Ichang. There was now only one course left, and that was to plan a thousand-mile journey and search the district where Father David had originally discovered the species thirty years or so ago. While turning over this plan, Wilson occupied his time collecting other plants from among the multitude growing in the district. Davidia had gone to the back of his mind. Then, on 19th May, when but a day or two's march from his headquarters, he saw a tree with something resembling huge white butterflies hovering among the branches. It was Davidia.

He at once arranged a careful search of the district, and as a result eleven more trees were found. They were watched carefully and with excitement until the seed was set. It was a difficult and dangerous period, for the Boxer rebellion was at its height and all foreigners in China were suspect. At last a rich harvest of seed was collected, sent to England, and finally successfully grown at Veitch's Coombe Wood nursery.

There are two pendants that may be hung on to this story which illustrate the luck and hazards of a plant-collector's life. During his later travels in China Wilson saw hundreds more Davidia trees, but never did he find them bearing seed as in the year of his first lucky encounter. And when he returned to England and saw his seedlings, he learned that during his absence it had become known that Farges had several years before sent seed to Maurice de Vilmorin, who had successfully raised plants in his nursery at Les Barres in France! There was, however, some consolation in the fact that de Vilmorin had only a few trees, while the firm of Veitch raised many thousands from Wilson's seed.

We must turn now and gain a more general idea of Wilson's other activities. His purpose, it must be remembered, was not botanical. It was to collect in good condition, and in as big quantities as possible, seeds of plants that would be likely to succeed and be popular in European gardens. The commercial firm of Veitch was footing the bill, and Wilson had to supply what they wanted. He had perforce to be an organiser whose aims were first to spot plants likely to be suitable for his purpose and secondly to ensure that plenty of seed or, when possible, roots or bulbs from them were collected at as little expense as possible. Thus he and his successors had a very different outlook from the French missionaries, Henry and their predecessors. Natives needed now to be trained to collect seeds, rather than specimens. All the same, most of these new plant-hunters happened to be keenly interested in natural history generally; they not only collected specimens but made copious notes in the field.

The results of his first trip of two years give an idea of Wilson's work. He brought or sent back the seeds of 305 species and 35 cases of bulbs and live roots. In addition, he collected and pressed specimens of 906 species. To catalogue the names of the trees and plants that became comparatively common in gardens as a result of his activities would be dull—maples, clematis, rhododendrons and viburnums now well known to us were among his collection. He also took very many excellent and valuable photographs (and cameras, complete with tripod stands and using glass plates for negatives, were far from the simple instruments of today).

Wilson went to China for Veitch once more in 1903. His plans were carefully laid in advance. If, for instance, it was necessary to make several visits to one particularly rich collecting area in order that he might be there at the different seasons of flowering and fruiting, he would usually approach it by a different and often circuitous route each time. By this means he covered a vast area of ground. On one occasion this practice nearly brought about his death and that of his party. Having planned to follow an unknown but possibly interesting track through difficult country, he found himself in a practically uninhabited district. The weather was appalling, and the few people there were on the verge of starvation. Wilson and his team also nearly starved to death, but just pulled through.

In 1905 he returned to England, with perhaps a rather less exciting haul than on his first trip. It was now his intention to settle down in England as a botanist. But he had not long taken up a post at the Imperial Institute when his friend Sargent came into the picture again. The American professor had been impressed by Wilson when they met at the beginning of the quest for Davidia. He had followed his successful career closely, and now asked him to go to China and collect plants for the Arnold Arboretum.

Wilson, after visiting the United States, arrived back in China. He was now able to work with greater freedom and more in accordance with his own interests. Sargent had a wide and practical knowledge of the Chinese situation and plants. He was the first director of the Arboretum, which had been founded as a part of Harvard University in 1872, and was busily engaged in making the collection of trees and shrubs as complete as possible. Long before, he had realised that a great many of the trees and shrubs of western China would grow in the climate of Boston—indeed, that they would thrive over much of the United States. The botanical aspect of plant-hunting rather than the purely commercial therefore came to the fore again; this appealed to Wilson's tastes, and so did the fact that Sargent was primarily interested in woody plants. These, along with bulbs, particularly lilies, had always attracted him more than herbaceous plants. Above all, the Arboretum authorities gave him a freer hand than Veitch. Thus he was now able to take greater chances and go where he considered there might be good collecting grounds.

This trip for the Arboretum proved an important one. A fine harvest of seed was collected. He was able, for instance, to visit—and be the first to collect in—the Mupin district, which had once been the centre of Father David's activities. He also made the first crossing of a dreadful land of wilderness, the Laolin—perhaps the only European to do so. For seventy miles the party tried to follow little-used tracks through this desolate country. But as they had been washed away by torrential rains, he was only able to keep his bearings by wading for miles along the margins of streams. Rain and mist were ceaseless. At no time during the journey was he able to see more than fifty paces through the gloom.

In 1910 he was once more back in China, again working for Sargent. His collecting fields on this expedition lay mostly in difficult and mountainous country. Yet in the valleys, during June and July (he

wrote), one could walk for days through veritable wild gardens
dominated by lilies. And one of these lilies that he collected on this
trip forms his monument in thousands of gardens. For it was here that he
found the Royal Lily, *Lilium regale*. Hundreds of bulbs were carefully
dug from the sun-baked rock crevices in which they grew. Shortly after
came disaster. A huge landslide crashed down without warning from
the mountains. Wilson, in his sedan chair, was hurled hundreds of feet
down the steep slope towards the river below. He struggled clear of the
tumbling chair, only to be struck by a boulder. One of his legs was
smashed. A tripod arm from his camera was made to serve as a rough
splint, and the long and painful trek back to civilisation began. The leg
was badly set, and for a time it seemed that it must be amputated. But
back in America the skill of a surgeon saved it, though for the rest of his
life a limp reminded him of the valley where dwells *Lilium regale*.

Other and easier journeys were made later. To Japan, for instance,
where he studied and became enthusiastic about the ornamental
cherries. Here, too, he sought out the city of Kurume on the island of
Kyushu, where, for over a century, gardeners had evolved the evergreen
dwarf Kurume azaleas, with their brilliant flowers. He also travelled
and collected in practically unknown islands in the Japanese Sea, in
Korea and in Formosa. Always, owing to his happy way with the inhabitants, he seemed to be taken to hitherto unvisited spots and allowed to
visit forbidden places. Soon he became Assistant Director of the Arnold
Arboretum, and when Sargent died, succeeded him as its Keeper.

Then, in 1930, after a life in which he had so many times defied
most of the dangers of nature, and sometimes the enmity of man, he
was killed in a motor accident in Massachusetts.

It is sad to relate, too, that the firm of Veitch came to an end just
as his finest introductions were coming into flower and maturity.
Neglected, they were grubbed up and burnt, or sold off cheaply. It
must be admitted that America set the true value on the man and his
works long before his own countrymen.

GEORGE FORREST

The name that is always linked with Wilson is that of George Forrest.
Though a slightly older man, he did not make his first trip to China

until five years after Wilson's. He continued his collecting, however, until after Wilson's death. The area in which he collected was further south, and the plants that he brought back are mostly not so hardy and therefore many of them have not become as popular and widely grown as those introduced by Wilson.

Forrest's early days take us back once more to that home of gardeners, Scotland. He was born in March 1873 at Falkirk. After a schooling at Kilmarnock Academy, he started work in a chemist's shop. This was hardly the life for an adventurous youth, but in later years it was to be of importance to him. For while there he learned something of the correct use of medicines, first aid and the elementary surgery of everyday life—all valuable assets for a traveller. As a trained pharmacist, too, he had to learn something of botany. Forrest seems to have been particularly interested in this part of his training, for he made a herbarium of local plants.

After a time he found that a lifetime spent in a chemist's shop was not his idea of a career. So off he went to Australia. Tree-felling, hard riding and life in the young country suited him. In the course of a year or two the chemist's assistant changed into a hardy and toughened man. But while the life was good, Australia at that time did not offer him much of value in the future. After a short stay in South Africa, he returned to Edinburgh.

He had kept an interest in plants. Among the applications that he now made for work was one to Sir Isaac Bayley Balfour at Edinburgh Botanic Garden—then, as we have seen, beginning to take notice of the riches of China. There was no job of any consequence available. A junior post in the Herbarium was, however, offered him if he cared to take it on the chance of something better coming along later. Fortunately he did.

From the arduous open-air life of the Australian bush, Forrest changed to the stuffy Herbarium, his days spent stooping over dried and pressed specimens. And now we see an early example of the energy and vigour of the man. To keep fit, he walked each day morning and evening to work from his home six miles out of Edinburgh. And all day he stood, making it a rule never to sit, at his work.

This stop-gap job proved in the end even more valuable to him than his training at the chemist's. He handled and sorted thousands of plants from all over the world. By doing so he gained a wide

Gentiana sino-ornata, the autumn-flowering blue gentian, introduced from China by George Forrest

knowledge of the world's plants and the characteristics by which they were classified.

Forrest was a keen sportsman—shooting, fishing, hill-climbing and gardening occupied his spare time. Towns he hated, and games left him uninterested.

In 1904, when he was thirty-one, came his chance. A. K. Bulley, of Neston in Cheshire, who was interested in a firm of nurserymen in Liverpool, believed in the possibilities of Chinese plants. Mr. Bulley was prepared to pay the cost of a plant-hunting expedition, and asked his friend Sir Isaac Bayley Balfour if he could recommend a collector. Forrest was chosen, and for the rest of his life plant-collecting, particularly in and around the province of Yunnan, was to be his work.

We do not know nearly as much about his day-to-day life as of many other explorers, for he wrote little of his travels at the time. Perhaps he had intended to recount the story during his retirement. But unhappily this never came, for he died at the finish of his last journey. His friends and colleagues have, however, done their best to fill the gap. From the results of their studies, and from a few articles and the letters that he wrote, we have a fair picture of the man at his work.

Though a plant-collector and botanist above all, Forrest belonged to the tradition of David Douglas—born adventurer, explorer and all-round naturalist. There was one big difference. While most previous plant-collectors worked as individuals, perhaps with the occasional help of a few natives, Forrest developed his inborn genius for organisation and for training others to work for him. At times he employed dozens of men, all working carefully and precisely to his instructions, collecting seeds and specimens. The quantities and variety of both that he sent home were enormous. For example, he sent home over thirty thousand botanical specimens from Yunnan. They were all dried and pressed with consummate skill, bearing concise descriptive notes about the living plants. How many packets of seed came from him (all equally carefully annotated) is not, so far as I can find, recorded.

The area over which he worked so efficiently covered about fifty thousand square miles. Nearly all this country was difficult and mountainous, so he had to plan his journeys with meticulous detail, and arrange either for himself or his trained men to be in a certain spot at just the right moment of flowering or harvest. He had in addition to meet continued upsets to his timetable caused by the dreadful weather in these hills, which strangely enough benefits their wonderful natural flower gardens.

In the summer of 1905 Forrest had been high up among the headwaters of the giant Mekong River, staying in the village of Tseku, near the borders of Tibet. Here he used as his headquarters one of the French mission stations, where lived two elderly priests and a few Chinese Christian converts.

The Tibetans were even more zealous in keeping foreigners out of their land than the Chinese. The expedition made by Colonel Younghusband to Lhasa, the most secret and holiest of their cities, had just taken place. It had greatly upset the governing sect of priests, or lamas, who controlled the country. These lamas also considered that the Chinese were encroaching on their territory. Their practical reaction was to wage war on all foreigners within striking distance. From time to time they would surround the small Chinese posts on their borders and murder all the inhabitants—Chinese and French missionaries alike. The lamas were particularly anxious to destroy these Christians, for the work of the French missionaries tended to undermine their despotic and brutal rule over the common people.

On a July evening news came through to the Tseku mission that the lamas had totally destroyed a small force of Chinese troops in a neighbouring town; their brutal gang would undoubtedly move next to Tseku, for the sole purpose of wiping out the village and its missionaries with their terrified little band.

Defence of the mission houses was impossible—only Forrest and the two brave old missionaries could use firearms. Immediate flight to a village thirty miles down the river, where lived a friendly chief with a strong force of Chinese troops, was therefore planned.

As the moon rose that night the party set out secretly. The two old priests rode on mules; Forrest and the native Christians walked.

The path was narrow and dangerous. On one side the ground dropped away to the rumbling, flooded Mekong River; on the other it rose high up to the snowy peaks of the mountains bordering the valley.

As the nervous party moved slowly through the dark, a signal whistle shrilled high above the roaring of the torrent. The lamas had arrived and the escape was discovered; the hunt was now on.

At dawn in the next village, Forrest learned that a force of the enemy, by a daring march, had now blocked the pathway further downstream. Escape seemed impossible, but the risk was taken and the party moved on.

Early in the afternoon a spot was reached where the path climbed high enough to give a view over the surrounding country. Forrest turned and looked back. In the clear light he saw smoke rising from the ruins at Tseku—and then, along the path which he had just passed, came a large armed band of pursuers, running at full speed in single file. Escape was now impossible; all were in the trap.

Old Father Bourdonnec rode off wildly on his mule. A shower of poisoned arrows brought him down; Tibetan double-handed swords finished the work. Nearly all the party of eighty either met the same fate as they fled or, even worse, were captured.

Forrest was well armed. He quickly turned and ran down a side path, out of range of his pursuers. Rounding a bend, he found a heavily armed force of the enemy stationed to cut off his escape. Should he try and shoot his way through them? He calculated that to do so was unwise. Letting himself be seen, he doubled back on his tracks—seemingly straight into the arms of the pursuing party.

But the moment he had rounded a bend and was out of sight of both forces, he leaped off the path. Down the steep bank he rolled, falling into dense jungle. His clothes were nearly stripped from his back; he was bruised and shaken. Crawling behind a boulder, he prepared his firearms to make a final stand.

He watched the troop that had blocked his way come rushing along the path above him in pursuit. They did not spot his ruse, and dashed on. He was safe for a time.

At darkness Forrest came out of hiding. He must now attempt to break away to the south. Out in the open, however, he soon saw that he was ringed in by his enemies. All around were parties of the lama's troops, with watchfires lit; in the flickering light he saw crouched their Tibetan man-hunting mastiffs, famed in the days of Marco Polo.

Eight hopeless days and nights of hide and seek followed. His only food was a handful of dried peas and a few heads of wheat carelessly dropped by the lamas. His boots had to be buried deep in a stream, for their marks disclosed his tracks. One day Forrest waded a mile through water to avoid his hunters; on another, their poisoned arrows passed through his hat. Once, while sleeping under a log on a river bed, he was woken by the voices of a band of thirty of his pursuers in full war paint crossing close by.

Then: "I knew the end was near, and determined to make one more bid for life," he later wrote.

The first move was to attempt a hold-up of a small cluster of huts, and to demand food at the gun-point. Happily, the natives proved friendly and took him in. Their only food was coarsely ground grain; of it he ate ravenously and almost died from the effects.

Forrest afterwards said that the headman of this little village was one of the best friends he had ever had. He was by now the sole object of the Tibetans' search; to hide him from their murderous bands was to take a fearful risk. But the headsman sheltered him until he was strong enough to travel to the next village. Here, guides were arranged to take him to safety over hidden paths crossing the high mountain-range.

This journey proved to be one of unbelievable misery. It was the middle of the wet season and ceaseless torrential rain poured down relentlessly. There was no shelter. No fires could be lit. Up and up they climbed, cutting their way through mile after mile of rhododendron thicket, dragging wearily over alps clothed with primulas, gentians, saxifrages and lilies. At last the snow-covered backbone of the range—17,000 feet high—was reached. A few handfuls of parched barley was their only food. Along the icy ridge they marched for six days, over glaciers and jagged rocks that wounded Forrest's feet.

Then, hoping that they were now outside the Tibetan cordon, the little band turned downhill. The descent was as difficult as the climb had been. On reaching the inhabited world again another disaster occurred. The natives protect their maize fields with sharply pointed bamboo spikes hidden in the ground. Forrest trod on one of these; it passed between the bones of his foot and speared out from the upper surface. The pain was agonising, and the wound took long to heal.

At last safety was reached. In the final stages Forrest had been disguised as a Tibetan. He was greeted by his friends as one who had returned from the dead. All that he had taken with him was lost—stores, camera, guns, camping equipment and, of course, his collections. All that remained were the rags in which he was clothed, his rifle, a revolver and two belts of cartridges.

Next we can illustrate the true measure of the man, his courage and his determination. This dreadful experience had befallen him in the valley of the Mekong River. Running parallel, often but a few miles away, is another great river valley, that of the Salween. This, too, runs up into Tibet; no white man had ever travelled up it. In October of the same year, barely three months after the massacre at Tseku, Forrest set out to make a journey towards its source, passing near to Tseku and penetrating yet further into Tibet. This daring journey was one of pure exploration—it was not the plant-hunting season. Forrest and his companion, Consul Litton (remembered by *Primula littoniana*, which grows in rockeries) became the first Europeans to gaze over hundreds of square miles of the great mountain system where rise the vast rivers of India and China. Although there were no thrilling adventures, conditions in the river valley were unhealthy; Litton fell ill and died shortly after his return. Forrest himself was later to suffer from the consequences of fever caught on this trip when during the following year he was plant-hunting and became seriously ill. This illness showed the success of his new methods, for his trained collectors continued to work efficiently while he lay on his sickbed.

Forrest's later trips were particularly concerned with the collection of rhododendrons. Some of them were financed by a Cornish enthusiast for these shrubs, J. C. Williams of Caerhays Castle. There are, of course, hundreds of different kinds of rhododendrons, ranging from tiny health-like shrubs to large trees with huge leaves. Forrest, largely at the behest of Williams, himself introduced over 300 new species and varieties. By so doing he gave the botanists something to argue over for many years to come, as well as the gardener some fine new shrubs.

His letters to his patron give some idea of the conditions of the district in which he was then working. Revolutions and risings were an everyday occurrence; at one place, 250 people out of a population of 5,000 were executed without trial; another village close by his camp was burned out and most of the people murdered; a debased coinage was issued and prices rose fantastically.

"Living in China," he wrote, "is like camping alongside an active volcano."

Yet, though often disheartened and sometimes temporarily defeated by weather, illness and other difficulties, his collections increased and he triumphed at his chosen task. In one thing he failed. He believed there was a centre of the rhododendron world, where unbelievable riches would be found. But this fabulous spot was never discovered; nor have any of his successors lighted upon it.

In 1930 began his last expedition. On its conclusion he wrote that he had succeeded in collecting "everything I wished for, and that means a lot . . . I have made a rather glorious and satisfactory finish to all my past years of labour."

Shortly after, while out shooting on 5th January, 1932, he called out to his servant as he fell in a faint. Within a few moments he was dead.

Hundreds of plants, particularly rhododendrons, that Forrest brought out of Asia for the first time are his memorial. Many, it is true, thrive only in the mild and moist western counties—in Cornwall, Devon, Wales and the stormy coastlands of western Scotland. But his finding of *Gentiana sino-ornata* in 1904, and introduction of it in 1910, brought a dazzling new plant to gardens all over the country. As its clear blue flowers fearlessly challenge the autumn and its threat of approaching winter, we must surely be reminded of the man of courage who brought it to us.

CHAPTER 12

Pioneers of the Present

We have seen in an earlier chapter the kind of garden that was beginning to evolve in Britain from the examples set by J. C. Loudon and Sir Joseph Paxton. The developments that took place in gardens were in many ways not quite what Paxton would have liked, and certainly Loudon would have had strong objections to many of them. William Kent, Lancelot Brown and Humphry Repton, we can feel certain, were turning in their graves, their spirits distraught by the lack of taste shown by the Victorian gardener.

For one thing, the pendulum again swung right over to the other side: colour, and garish colour at that, came into full favour once more. While the study of nature—and, of course, plants—on scientific lines progressed by leaps and bounds, "nature" in the sense understood by all the gardeners from Kent to Loudon went right out of fashion. First of all we must blame the new school of practical gardeners; these men were exceedingly skilful at cultivating plants. And next we must accuse the greenhouse. From the eighteen-twenties onwards these had improved remarkably in efficiency and popularity until in Paxton's later years they became among the most important features in gardens. Their cost fell considerably, and a whole new class of society—and a class with neither tradition nor very refined tastes—could now own them. Then there were all the new plants coming from overseas at an ever-increasing rate now that steamers had made transport so much easier. Particularly popular were tender plants suitable for growing in the new greenhouses. Finally, I think that we should mention the fall in the cost of building by the introduction of "sham" substitutes for expensive materials, and an increase by mass production of garden ornaments. All these things seemed marvellous to the Victorians. They took all that was offered to them, thoughtlessly and unimaginatively. One result was the most usual feature of Victorian gardening—"bedding-out". Flower-beds, in all sorts of fancy shapes, remained empty in winter and spring until the weather was mild enough to bring from their warm frames and greenhouses a host of plants that would only live out-of-doors when there was no chance of a frost. Into the beds they were then put, arranged in elaborate geometrical patterns. This form of gardening is still carried on to a modest extent. (And charming it is too, in strict moderation.) But as Victoria's long reign progressed, bedding-out more and more filled the flower-gardens; it became an unimaginative ritual. Oddly coloured rocks and pieces of coloured spa, striking jaggedly into the air, ornate and usually badly made artificial stone ornaments, and tropical sea-shells added to the strange effect.

The greenhouses in the meantime remained full of even more exotic plants throughout the summer.

All the traditional forms of English gardening about which we have written disappeared from every garden that aspired to be in the fashion—as well as many of the old plants. The vegetable and fruit garden were, however, raised to a state of perfection unknown before. Labour was abundant, and hosts of underpaid but highly skilled gardeners, working from early in the morning to late at night, produced these strange and extravagant results; only in the unfashionable cottage and poor man's garden did the true plants and spirit of the English garden remain secreted.

WILLIAM ROBINSON

William Robinson was born in Ireland in 1839. J. C. Loudon was then still alive. He was a young man when Paxton died. During his youth and early days the worst features of the Victorian garden grew overwhelmingly triumphant. When he died, a little short of a century old, the Victorian garden had gone for ever, destroyed by its enemies, of whom he was the leader.

He was a remarkable character. Considering his numerous acquaintances, the many visitors to his own garden, the vast number of words that he wrote for his very successful publications, we know surprisingly little about the man himself. On the other hand, of his theories and work we know everything.

His life-story is simple. He was secretive about his parents and childhood, first appearing on the scene as a humble garden-boy working on the big estate of an Irish clergyman-baronet. He was clearly intelligent and keen, for at twenty-one he was in charge of the range of greenhouses. We can imagine the number of tender and rare plants that furnished them, after the fashion of Chatsworth, and the numerous seedlings and cuttings they harboured to be brought forward for furnishing the flower-beds when summer came. Everything was grown to the height of perfection—until one bitter winter night in 1861. During the day previously, the young foreman had some violent disagreement with his employer (or so it seems; no one knows exactly what happened). So that night, as the thermometer, always watched by Robinson so carefully, fell first to freezing and then below, he went to the stokehole and drew out the fires. Then after walking round the houses and opening all the windows, he set out for Dublin, arriving there early on the following morning.

This manner of beginning a highly successful career—for his employer's plants were at once frozen to death—is, to say the least, extraordinary, and certainly quite unlike any of Robinson's predecessors in this book. Even more odd is the fact that when he called upon the Director of the Royal Botanic Gardens at Glasnevin, who apparently knew all about the greenhouse incident, that eminent botanist and gardener gave him an introduction to the Curator of the Royal Botanic Society's garden in London. From this we can only presume that there was a good deal to be said in Robinson's defence.

At the Botanic Society's gardens he obtained work and was soon a foreman once more. He was, perhaps purposely, not put in charge of greenhouses, but of the beds of hardy herbaceous plants. These included one section filled with English wild flowers, which soon had

Robinson's devoted attention. At week-ends he travelled widely in the home counties and even to the seashores beyond to collect new plants for it. So he came to love intensely the English countryside and its wild flowers. From this he "began to get an idea (which should be taught to every boy at school) that there was (for gardens even) much beauty in our native flowers and trees, and then came the thought that if there was so much in our own island, what might we not look for from the hills and valleys of the northern and temperate world?"

These ideas developed slowly, but they began to be formed at the time when the highest taste in gardening was considered to be the Crystal Palace, reçently moved into the Surrey countryside at Sydenham, with its water temples, water paths, stone basins—poor imitations of Italian models—furnished with tens of thousands of plants brought out from the greenhouses for each summer and neatly placed in the elaborate pattern of flower-beds. Even the smallest and poorest garden tried to ape this Crystal Palace manner: "I saw," wrote Robinson, "the flower-gardener meanly trying to rival the tile or wall-paper man." Before long he had resolved on an attempt to replace all this artificiality by seeking to bring back into them "the spirit of natural beauty".

While these ideas were coming into the mind of the clever young gardener, he was working hard not only at his profession but in repairing the lack of education of his Irish youth. Before long his standard in botany was such that he was elected a Fellow of the learned Linnean Society; he learned to write good English and to speak French fluently and with an excellent accent.

Before he was thirty, having left the Botanic Society's garden (this time in the orthodox manner), he was in Paris at the Exhibition of 1867 as representative of the firm of Veitch, and on *The Times* newspaper as their horticultural correspondent.

As a journalist and writer, Robinson was at once a success. In 1869 appeared his first book, an account of French gardens, written following extensive travels in France. He also made an Alpine walking tour, and published *Alpine Flowers for English Gardens* in 1870—a year which we can say marks the beginning of the modern rock-garden.

Shortly after came *The Wild Garden*. In it he fired his first really heavy broadsides at the Victorian garden. The aim of this book was described in a sub-title, which proclaims that it will urge the naturalisation and natural grouping of *hardy* foreign plants and the use of British wild flowers. The frontispiece shows a combe in the west country planted with primroses, kingcups and daffodils; what a revolutionary idea in the days when greenhouses and bedding-out with echeverias, geraniums and calceolarias reigned supreme in the fashionable world!

Robinson soon gained ardent and intelligent disciples, who brought the first modern "natural" gardens into being.

"Nature", as we now see it through Robinson's eyes, is something quite different from the vision of "Capability" Brown or Repton. It is not the English countryside moulded and planted to resemble an idealised landscape painting, but the English countryside itself (perhaps even as left by "Capability" and now matured), with but a little alteration and clearing, no longer a "green thought" but planted with those flowering trees, shrubs and plants that will maintain themselves with but little trouble to the gardener.

Robinson worked on the same lines in the more formal parts of the garden which he held should lie round the house. Hardy and permanent plants replaced the annual "bedders". Large, simple lawns of turf—Britain's unique possession—covered up the many curiously shaped beds. The plants themselves lived in larger borders of honest, plain design. Jagged chunks of white spa that stuck spikily into the air were carted away and replaced by native English stone lying in gentle natural contours over which sprawled true alpine plants. The plaster imitations of Italian stone urns and basins were put away.

Robinson brought in this new vision of natural gardening not so much by practice in the manner of Kent and Brown, or later Paxton, but by his skill as journalist and editor. In this he compares with J. C. Loudon. (A remarkable achievement, too, for a man who was self-educated.) In 1871 was founded the first of his papers, *The Garden*, and later *Gardening Illustrated*. Since Loudon's time still another and larger class of amateur gardeners had arisen, with smaller gardens. It was for this new class that Robinson particularly edited and wrote. Thereby he made money, which he invested profitably and wisely. By 1884 he had saved enough to buy a two-hundred-acre estate in Sussex lying round the Elizabethan manor of Gravetye. Here he spent the rest of his long life, never ceasing to alter and improve the house and gardens and bring them into accord with his own ideas of the perfect English garden. Gravetye, together with the offices of his papers, became the headquarters of the new movement in gardening.

In the meantime, Robinson had given advice on the planning or alteration of a number of gardens. His method of working was different from that of his predecessors. He marked out the design *on* the ground itself. He insisted that each part of the plan, however small, must be dictated by the lie of the land and even its soil. Existing trees, plants and buildings must all be taken into account. You could, he said, make a plan of a garden on paper after it had been laid out, but never before; paper plans in advance were useless theory, no more.

A great triumph for his campaign occurred in the early eighteen-eighties. For many miles round, the ornate tower of Shrublands is seen as a landmark rising above the ancient wooded park that surrounds it; the equally fanciful lodges are passed on more than one road that approaches Ipswich nearby. Once the site of an ancient house, the popular Victorian architect Sir Charles Barry (who designed the Houses of Parliament) reared an opulent and elaborate building, surrounded by fifty acres of garden of equal complexity. Forty gardeners kept it tidied and "bedded out". Summer after summer the bedding in front of the house, curling in scrolls and dotted with fanciful shapes, was planted with thousands of brightly coloured plants. Winding and narrow paths of grass, or of gravel, sand and coloured brick, chopped up the surface of the ground into a thousand fragments; yellow, red and blue stones provided coloured ornament. Shrublands garden was not only an East Anglian wonder, but, in Robinson's own words, a centre and example of the bedding-out cult for the whole of Britain. Not a creeper trailed over the elaborate stonework of the house to soften its bare condition, not a slender spray of ivy was allowed to linger for a moment out of place—yet in this strange perfection of a garden there could not be found a single spray of flowers that might be used to decorate a room! Then Robinson was called in.

He swept away the niggling little beds and replaced them with lawns. Their calm green showed off the variety of the planting in the simplified borders, where now grew perennial plants that stayed in place for years. Other beds were filled with shrubs, in particular roses. Climbing plants, such as flowering wistarias and clematis, were allowed to ramble over the buildings and hide the hard angles of its stonework.

Shrublands Park became once again a famed example—but now of the Robinsonian type of garden—and one that more than any other sounded the death-knell of the "pastry-cook's garden".

In 1883 was first issued Robinson's most successful book, *The English Garden*. This is described by its long sub-title: "Design and Arrangement shown by existing examples of Gardens in Great Britain and Ireland followed by a Description of the best Plants for the Open-air Garden and their Culture." This great work has gone through edition after edition. The second part, containing descriptions of hardy flowers, flowering shrubs, trees, evergreens and ferns, is the true successor to the works by Miller and Loudon. It is a practical book, describing the cultivation of the plants, and how to place them properly in the garden, and contains the valued work of many of Robinson's colleagues who were specialists in different kinds of plants.

The rest of his life was spent editing, writing, gardening—and quarrelling. Robinson was, in fact, a bit of a crank and had several bees in his bonnet. Greenhouses and greenhouse plants were understandably one; within a few years he had removed them all from Gravetye. Bedding-out, of course, was another: even the little that was still done at Kew, harmless enough, caused him to wage war on that fine garden and its great director the second Hooker. Another bone of contention with Kew was that the plants were labelled with the Latin botanical names; Robinson passionately believed that every plant should be given an English name—which we can now see to be a sheer impossibility. Then he disliked all the conifers that came from the Pacific coast of America, in particular Wellingtonias and the discoveries of David Douglas. He called them foreigners unsuited to our landscape—yet he admired and planted thousands of Corsican pines and larch, just as foreign to our scene! He was, indeed, not a very reasonable man when it came to his prejudices. But there is no doubt that we owe to him the revival of all that was best in the traditions of English gardening after half a century of eclipse. And we owe to him, also, the way of gardening that has been most successful not only in this country but in North America, in suiting present-day conditions when labour is scarce.

As the years passed Robinson prospered; he steadily completed the revolution in our gardens, helped by an increasingly large band of friends, who included some of the cleverest and most knowledgeable gardeners of all times. The Irish garden-boy eventually grew into a wealthy English country squire—even if he did not become Lord Lieutenant of his adopted county of Sussex, as "Capability" had.

At seventy-two he lost the use of his legs; the development of motor transport (which he pretended to despise) soon provided him with a little caterpillar-tracked vehicle that would carry him to the most remote part of his estate. At ninety-five he set about planting a new orchard; at ninety-seven, shortly before he died, he was in London to visit an exhibition of pictures (he was something of a connoisseur). We read that his last words at the end of his long and fruitful life were, "Children are always delightful"—yet Robinson had never married, and we cannot help thinking that in his heart of hearts he really considered plants more delightful than any other living thing.

GERTRUDE JEKYLL

If, in the late eighteen-seventies, one had visited the office in London from which William Robinson published his papers, one might have met a very hale and hearty woman—very different from the type of frail, dependent women that so many people believe to have been usual in Victoria's reign. Gertrude Jekyll was one of Robinson's keenest disciples, though holding very decided opinions of her own.

We have mentioned before that gardening draws together people of remotely different social positions; here is another instance. Miss Jekyll was probably Robinson's closest friend. Yet the two could scarcely have differed more in their ancestry and upbringing. Of Robinson's origins and early days practically nothing is known; education he himself acquired in the intervals of making a living.

On the other hand, members of the Jekyll family can be found recorded among the gentlefolk, lawyers, clergy, soldiers, sailors and servants of the Crown over centuries. Never really wealthy, yet they owned good estates. One only achieved any particular fame, and a knighthood, Sir Joseph Jekyll, a Master of the Rolls in the early eighteenth century. He earns a special mention, too, from the fact that he was responsible for the erection or restoration of no less than thirty-nine houses or buildings.

Miss Jekyll's own father was a retired captain in the Grenadier Guards; her mother, the daughter of a banker. She was born in 1843 (the very year in which J. C. Loudon died), one of a large family. When she was five, the Jekylls left London and settled in a big, dignified, comfortable-looking house near Guildford in Surrey. It was here that she began her country childhood, a period of happy and fully occupied years. She became a strong and active girl, much preferring boyish pastimes to those usually considered suitable to the daughter of a Victorian household. Her father delighted in making things, and with the other children she had the run of a good workshop. Here they learned to handle tools properly and skilfully, often from the clever old country craftsmen. Captain Jekyll was interested in science, too, and Gertrude, with her skilful fingers, used to help him in his electrical experiments.

The garden had a pool, a spot for many adventures. They used as a boat a large discarded wooden beer-cooler, a box-like affair; it was quite unsafe, indeed dangerous, but no harm resulted—only such pleasures as gudgeon freshly caught and fried for tea.

When her brothers went to school, Gertrude was often alone, and it was then that she learned to know flowers as individual beings. She learned that not only did they possess their own personal appearances and colours, but other qualities just as important, such as their scent and feel to the touch when handled. From these days of her childhood, therefore, she knew a multitude of wild and garden flowers as close friends long before she learned their names. (She could, for instance, often recognise trees at night from the sound made by the sighing of the wind in their branches.)

Hours were spent watching and talking with the working people of the district, the last generations of craftsmen that within a few years disappeared, to be replaced by machinery. These old people with the inherited skills in their hands (which often died within them) gave the children, already brought up by their father in a tradition of good workmanship, immense delight. They accounted for Gertrude's lifelong enthusiasm for objects of all kinds that were well-made by hand from first-rate materials. This was an important element in all that she did and wrote. Later in life she described in a book, *West Surrey: Some Notes and Memories*, many of these old characters that she had known, admired and had fortunately photographed before it was too late.

As a contrast to these quiet and intimate country adventures and pursuits, wealthy neighbours from time to time took the excited children in style to the London theatre and to the races. Summer holidays were spent at sea in the family yacht, or later (when the boat became too small for them) in travelling on the Continent.

Then there was music, too. Mrs. Jekyll was a clever pianist and other members of the family circle talented musicians—one of the boys, Walter, became a teacher of singing and was a pioneer in the appreciation of Wagner's music.

As Gertrude grew up and left behind this happy and varied childhood, she devoted more and more time to the arts of painting, drawing and designing, and decided to become a professional artist. She went to the South Kensington School of Art, and was early marked as an exceptionally promising student. Before long she achieved some success as a painter. But other interests and friendships called her; she was a sociable girl, with friends such as Ruskin, Watts and an eminent archaeologist at the British Museum. With the last and his family she made a long trip to the East. She was particularly interested in gilding, too, and visited Italy to study under a master of that craft.

She began to do well in her career: a picture was hung at the Royal Academy, but more important was her success as a designer. Among other commissions, she designed furnishings for the Duke of Westminster's seat at Eaton Hall in Cheshire.

All the time she had remained interested in gardens and plants. The journals that she kept while on her travels abroad often make knowledgeable references to them. She early threw in her lot with William Robinson and his movement, and in the eighteen-seventies began a friendship with him that lasted her life; from that time, too, she wrote regularly for his papers.

In the meantime the family had left Surrey and gone to live in the Thames valley. When Captain Jekyll died, however, Mrs. Jekyll decided to return to Surrey, and build a house for herself at Munstead, then a remote and isolated spot on bare heathland. Miss Jekyll was in her element, giving of her best in helping with the design of the house and its furnishings and particularly with laying out the garden. This started to play a much more important part in her life; her mother's new home began to receive many famous gardeners, in addition to artists and musicians who had always been frequent visitors. Before long, indeed, the Munstead garden became known far beyond the Surrey borders, and its maker began occasionally to advise and plan for other gardeners. The first garden that she ever designed was for a factory lad at Rochdale who wanted his little plot as full of good and inexpensive plants as possible. On the other hand, she helped such eminent men as G. F. Wilson, who was then laying out the estate at Wisley, which later became the garden of the Royal Horticultural Society.

Not far from Munstead lived the Lutyens family. A son, Edwin, who was much younger than Miss Jekyll, had embarked on his career as architect. With her, he had a profound respect for the old traditional methods of building and the loving use of good materials. The two had much else in common and before long Miss Jekyll was giving him hints and suggestions for planning the gardens around the houses that he was now designing.

Yet, although she was becoming quite famous in the gardening world, this branch of her work remained little more than a hobby for several years to come; her true career was that of designer and craftswoman.

Then, in 1891, she suffered a bitter blow. Her eyes were troublesome, to continue with painting, drawing, embroidery and other such activities would, she was warned, result in blindness. So she devoted herself to gardening and garden design; before long began a professional and fruitful partnership with Lutyens.

After her mother's death, Miss Jekyll decided to build her own house also at Munstead. Edwin Lutyens was naturally the architect. In 1896 Munstead Wood, as the place was called, began to rise; Miss Jekyll moved in the next year, just after the Royal Horticultural Society had presented to her their Victoria Medal of Honour, awarded only to those few who have given outstanding service to the art or craft of gardening.

Munstead Wood and its garden are probably even more important in the history of gardening than Stowe with all its fame and magnificence. For whereas the landscape garden of Bridgeman and his successors resulted in the completion of perhaps hundreds of gardens, or rather estates, in the "landscape" style, the example of Munstead Wood has been followed in many thousands of instances, not only in the British Isles but in North America, where Miss Jekyll soon had many followers. It is a style, of course, that can reach perfection in an acre or two, or even less, and therefore from a practical point of view well suited to the present day.

Miss Jekyll was inspired by William Robinson, the mastermind and the master-gardener of the new kind of gardens. But he was not the trained, skilled and sensitive artist that she was. Robinson developed the simply-shaped border using hardy, more or less permanent plants, but it was Miss Jekyll who, with her understanding of the use of form and colour, mastered after much of a lifetime devoted to their study, turned it into a work of art, subtle in colour and shape of flower and foliage alike. Her training, too, made her a pioneer in reviving the art of flower arrangement in houses. Her close friendship with Sir Edwin Lutyens, as he became, and their joint understanding and sympathetic use of building materials—of bricks, stone, timber—enabled her to perceive far more acutely than Robinson the right relationship of a garden and its plants to the house that it encircled.

She worked during a period when a vast number of new hardy plants, trees and shrubs were coming into our gardens, both from overseas and from the nurseries of the plant-breeders. Here again, her artist's training and long practical experience of gardening were of great importance in setting a standard, and in ensuring that gardeners chose only the best from all the novelties that flooded in upon them, while retaining all that was good among the old favourites. Her work will be better understood from a reading of her book about the building and planting of Munstead Wood, *Home and Garden*. From it may be learned also something of her friends the craftsmen and old characters of Surrey, of her many cats and their lives and adventures, of her dislike of rich people who gardened only through "hirelings"—and a lot else about this remarkable woman.

Miss Jekyll designed over three hundred gardens. They ranged from the garden for the Queen's Doll's House to those surrounding the cemeteries of the men killed in the European war of 1914–18. The loveliest are those surrounding moderate-sized houses lying among the sandy heathlands where rhododendrons, red-stemmed pines and the delicate silver birches are at home; this was the kind of ground that she had learned to understand intimately at her Surrey homes.

She was herself a fine practical gardener, and patiently worked on producing strains of several kinds of plant—the Munstead polyanthus, for instance. In old age she felt it deeply when infirmity stopped her doing even little things in the garden with her own hands. She lived on to see a new age, which she did not like or understand—brightened though it occasionally was by some new plant brought into cultivation. In her ninetieth year she died; her master and oldest gardening friend, William Robinson, travelled to her funeral.

At least one fine portrait of Miss Jekyll was made, showing an obviously once rather severe but now mellowing old lady. Yet we may prefer to remember her by Sir William Nicholson's wonderful painting of her old and battered boots, of good honest workmanship, no doubt, but like their owner in more than due time worn out by gardening.

REGINALD FARRER

The last of our pioneers is surely the strangest character of them all. We have seen something of practical gardeners, both professionals and amateurs, botanists, architects, artists, plant-collectors and authors. So far as I know, Farrer never designed a building, but he was concerned with gardening both as amateur and professional, with botany, painting, writing—and died as a plant-hunter in a remote Burmese valley while in the midst of the seed harvest. He was also a Justice of the Peace, a County Councillor and had stood unsuccessfully for Parliament. Born long after Robinson and Miss Jekyll, with whose period and style his name will always be linked, they both outlived him.

Reginald Farrer was a north-countryman, born and brought up at the foot of Ingleborough, the remarkable limestone hill in Yorkshire where some of our rarest native alpine plants are found. He came of an old family, his father having been High Sheriff of the county. He went to no school—perhaps because of an infirmity—but no doubt received at home a better education than he would otherwise have done. In due course he followed his ancestors up to Balliol College, Oxford. From childhood he was interested in plants, particularly alpine plants, and made his first rock-garden when he was fourteen.

After leaving the university, he went touring in China, Japan and Canada. He published an account of this journey, which launched him on his career of author. Later, besides his important gardening and travel books, he published several others of different kinds, including novels—now, I fear, forgotten.

In 1907 he published *My Rock Garden*, and shortly after, a book on bog and water gardens. Both were written in an excited, enthusiastic manner, in prose that used the full melodious and colourful range of the English language. They marked the author as a cultured man of the world, yet something of a poet and artist. It was clear to those who read them that he knew a great deal about plants, both as they grew wild and as a gardener. Certainly no gardening books like them had ever been published before.

At that time rock-gardening and water-gardening were coming into fashion. They fitted well with the natural style of gardening preached by Robinson and Miss Jekyll, which was triumphing over the old bedding-out manner. The cultivation of rock-plants in rather peculiar rockeries had a long history; we have mentioned those made in ancient Mexico and that constructed out of bits of the Tower of London by Forsyth. But for the popularisation of the type of rock-garden designed to grow the true wild plants of the mountains in conditions resembling their native homes, we must again give most of the credit to William Robinson. Farrer, with his specialised knowledge and the purple passages of his prose, made these new rock-gardens in the naturalistic style.

He was, too, one of the first to bring a feeling of romance and a sense of adventure into rock-gardening—the new spirit that came about during the transformation scene when the Victorian rockery (which he called "the almond-pudding scheme"), with white pinnacles spiking up from a round bed, quite unsuitable for real rock-plants, was changed to our modern alpine-garden, where chosen plants from the mountains of Europe and China alike are often to be found growing as well as they do at home.

Farrer's attitude is well illustrated by the manner in which he attacked the "arch-imposter" of the Victorian rockery, edelweiss—the "Flannel flower of the Alps, so ridiculously sought after and marvelled at . . . far from being *the* typical alpine flower, it is not even an alpine plant at all . . ."; he goes on to describe how he has seen it growing like a daisy in level stretches, and that only by accident does it occasionally seed itself in inaccessible places—not because it is rare, but from its very adaptability.

The kind of plant that he and those who followed him sought, and the spirit of their quest, is summed up in these lines:

> "In and out of all the great mountain-chains lives *Eritrichium nanum*, but high, high up . . . so high that, except with luck, the mere walker can rarely hope to meet with it. Into chinks of the great granite precipices it makes its little cobweb cushions of down . . . hidden by the dense mass of its dazzling sky-blue blossoms."

A whole chapter is needed to describe the adventure of finding this rare plant, and, when found, of trying to grow it in the garden.

His books and articles excited and urged on his increasing number of followers; in them, they could travel with him in the alps of Europe or the valleys of China seeking plants, and read of the adventures great and small, serious and comic, which he encountered. Not a few, indeed, followed in his footsteps.

In 1912 Farrer began work on *The English Rock Garden*. This study of rock-gardens and rock-plants for British gardens was on a scale never attempted before or since. Its two big volumes, published nearly ten years later, became and remain the standard and most influential work on the subject. Not only was his extensive practical knowledge brought into play for the writing of this book, but he studies the literature about and dried specimens of alpine plants coming from parts of the world that he did not know. Possibly it was this rummaging among the floras and dried specimens that brought to him a realisation that upon the mountains of China there must be many fine alpine plants well suited to our own rockeries and still awaiting collection. The other travellers in those regions had brought home mostly trees, shrubs, bulbs and plants for more general use in gardens.

So in 1914 Farrer set out to visit Kansu and northern China, accompanied by William Purdom. These two made an odd pair. Farrer, stout and something of a man about town, always overflowing with energy and enthusiasm; talkative but afflicted with an impediment in his speech—an extravagant character. Purdom, on the other hand, was quiet and unassuming, already practised in Chinese plant-collecting, and so well able to handle the natives that he eventually became an inspector of forests under the Chinese government.

The expedition was a success, though unfortunately the war that had broken out in Europe caused the temporary neglect and even loss of a number of its introductions. None the less, we owe it to *Viburnum fragrans*, the winter-flowering guelder rose, which is now to be found in most gardens; *Buddleia alternifolia*, with long weeping-willow-like branches covered with lilac flowers, so unlike Father David's buddleia; the "threepenny-bit" rose, *Rosa farreri*; and a number of alpine plants. Farrer also made numerous paintings of Chinese plants growing in their mountain homes—not very good ones, it must be admitted.

On his return to an England depressingly at war, Farrer wrote two remarkable books about those two years in China. Written in his magnificent picturesque and rather exaggerated style, they far excel any other writings by plant-collectors and are fascinating to read. The first is *On the Eaves of the World*, the second *The Rainbow Bridge*.

Peace declared, Farrer set off again as soon as he was able. This time he chose the unexplored mountains of Upper Burma. His companion was E. H. M. Cox. Here the climate was bad and continuously stormy, though generally so warm that most of the plants that they collected eventually proved unsuitable for any but the mildest of British gardens. Nothing, however, daunted Farrer's excitement and enthusiasm for the unknown high places and the flowers. After the first season, Cox had to come back home. Farrer continued alone, going on into even more remote and unhealthy country. Here he made a fine collection of specimens of plants and, in the autumn, a big haul of seeds. In 1920 he wrote a letter home describing how his hut was full of paper trays on which were spread the seeds that he was trying to dry in the warm, wet and sunless climate. The seeds never came; the climate proved too much for this extraordinary and rather heroic man. He died on

17th October, 1920, among the remote mountains, alone with his native servants. A passage from his writings can suitably end this book.

"All the wars of the world, all the Caesars, have not the staying power of a lily in a cottage border . . . The immortality of marbles and of miseries is a vain, small thing compared to the immortality of a flower that blooms and is dead by dusk."

Some Books to Read

On coming to compile this list I was surprised to find how much of my information had been collected from often old or inaccessible periodicals, or as incidental matter in books about other subjects which had, over the years, caught my eye and been noted. Many of our pioneers still remain without a biography; the gaps in this short bibliography indicate possible subjects for writers of the future!

The books that follow include only those that are likely to be obtainable from a good public library.

The best general history is *The Story of Gardening* by Richardson Wright (1934), but it is now getting out of date.

CHAPTER I

A good book is wanted on ancient gardens. Otherwise we have only Sir Arthur Hort's translation of Theophrastus' *Enquiry Into Plants and Minor Works* (1916), which has copious notes; *The Greek Herbal of Dioscorides*, edited by R. T. Gunther (1934); and, most useful, *Herbals, Their Origin and Evolution*, by E. A. Arber (1938 edition).

CHAPTER II

Early British Botanists and Their Gardens, R. T. Gunther (1922). Selections from Goodyer's edition of Gerard's *The Herball* and Parkinson's writings have been published from time to time.

CHATPER III

For Le Nôtre and his times, see *Two Royal Domains of France*, D. McDougall (1931). For Henry Wise, there is *Gardener to Queen Anne*, David Green (1956).

CHAPTER IV

Oxford Gardens, R. T. Gunther (1912); *The Romance of the Apothecaries' Garden at Chelsea*, F. D. Drewett (1928); *The Prince of Botanists, Carl Linnaeus*, Norah Gourlie (1953).

CHAPTER V

The English Landscape Garden, H. F. Clark (1948); *The Work of William Kent*, Margaret Jourdain (1948); *Capability Brown*, Dorothy Stroud (1950). There is no study of Humphry Repton.

CHAPTER VI

The Royal Botanic Gardens, Kew, W. J. Bean (1908).

CHAPTER VII

Apart from *Sir Joseph Banks: The Aristocrat of the Philosophers*, H. C. Cameron (1952), reference must be made to articles by A. Simmonds scattered through the *Journal of the Royal Horticultural Society* from 1941 to 1944. (The same author's *A Horticultural Who Was Who* (1948) deals with several other minor figures not included here.)

CHAPTER VIII

The career of David Douglas remains as a splendid and untouched subject for a biographer. Earlier plant-hunting in America is described in *New Green World*, Josephine Herbst (1954). *The Coming of the Flowers*, A. W. Anderson (1950), deals shortly with a number of other plant-hunters. For China, we are fortunate to have *Plant Hunting in China*, E. H. M. Cox (1945). Some old libraries still possess Robert Fortune's own *Three Years Wandering in the Northern Provinces of China* (1847) and *Yedo and Peking: A Narrative of a Journey to the Capitals of Japan and China* (1863).

CHAPTER IX

Thomas Knight, his brother Richard and their circle remain fascinating subjects for some enterprising biographer. *The Life of Mendel*, Hugo Iltis (1932).

CHAPTER X

Some Nineteenth Century Gardeners, Geoffrey Taylor (1951), gives, among many other interesting things, the only recent account of Mr. and Mrs. Loudon; see also the same author's important *The Victorian Flower Garden* (1952). *Paxton and the Bachelor Duke*, Violet Markham (1935), is notable.

CHAPTER XI

E. H. M. Cox's own experiences give particular authenticity to the chapters on collectors of the present century in *Plant Hunting in China*. E. H. Wilson gave some account of his own work in *A Naturalist in Western China* (1913). *The Journeys and Plant Introductions of George Forrest*, edited by J. MacQueen Cowan (1952), is finely illustrated from Forrest's own photographs. See also any of numerous books written by F. Kingdon-Ward on his own (mostly later) experiences. Reginald Farrer's two masterpieces, *On the Eaves of the World* (1917) and *The Rainbow Bridge* (1921), really belong here.

CHAPTER XII

For William Robinson and the life of Farrer, see Geoffrey Taylor's *Some Nineteenth Century Gardeners*, which also discusses Miss Jekyll. But *Gertrude Jekyll: A Memoir*, Francis Jekyll (1931), gives a much fuller account of her.

NOTE

Several important pioneers as well as some of the minor characters can, of course, be looked up in *The Dictionary of National Biography*—though in some cases this is now out of date and often does not always tell as much about the gardening activities of those who have other claims to fame as we should like!

INDEX

Note:- Page numbers in italic refer to illustrations.